PIG BEACH BBQ

PIG BEACH BBQ

A NOTE FROM OUR FOUNDER

I have always loved to eat, drink, and entertain. And one of the best ways to do all three is cook with live fire in my own backyard. Living in Manhattan doesn't offer too many backyard spots, but those of us who can hightail it to the country or the beach every weekend to do just that. For years, weekends were my fun time as I gathered good friends and colleagues for fishing on my boat, the *Salty Rinse*, golf, and BBQ bashes at my place in Sag Harbor.

Feeding my love of good eats, I have been an investor in some of New York City's great restaurants, where it was my immense pleasure to get to know many of the city's amazing chefs. Del Posto, New York's four-star Italian restaurant where Matt Abdoo was chef de cuisine, was one of my favorites. I would often stop in for dinner and some restaurant gossip. I eventually got to know Matt very well and discovered that we had a common interest in backyard barbecue. I eventually invited him to join us at my beach house, where I did my weekend cooking. Although I focused on barbecue, Matt introduced some culinary tricks and restaurant recipes that added more fuel to my barbecue fire.

We had such a great time in the backyard that even before we knew what the future would hold, we were off on a trip to Texas Hill Country to learn what authentic Texas barbecue meant and how we could bring it to our backyard cooking. That became the impetus to turn our weekend hobby into serious tournament mode. So serious that together, our skills untried, we embarked on a BBQ adventure to the famous Memphis in May barbecue competition as the Salty Rinse Barbecue Team. With no Southern heritage and no authentic barbecue experience to back us up, we had an amazing year, finishing second in Whole Hog and first in Poultry.

Living a block away from Balthazar in Soho, I was a regular at the famed hot spot and became friendly with executive chef Shane McBride, but we had no idea our future paths would cross. Shane was also in the midst of realizing his dream of putting together an awesome crew of like-minded chefs to hone their backyard barbecue skills. When our team won first prize in Poultry and second prize in Whole Hog and Shane's team won, too, not only were we stunned, we were stunned into real hard-core action.

Who could have imagined that two of New York's most highly lauded chefs and one New York food lover would meet on the grounds of *the* major Southern barbecue competition, battling a mass of seasoned Southern pitmasters, and come up winners? From that point on, we kept entering—and frequently winning—competitions, first separately and then together. That was when we decided we needed a permanent spot to broaden our competitive edge.

On the hunt for our permanent location, I was introduced to what was considered an up-and-coming neighborhood on the banks of Brooklyn's Gowanus Canal. I was perplexed about what to call our new venture, but at that moment, it dawned on me that we could call it Pig Beach, an ode to the swimming pigs of Exuma, in the Bahamas, a spot I have visited frequently on my boat. The rest was history! Pig Beach, our Brooklyn barbecue restaurant, was born, first as an open-air pop-up and then as a year-round indoor-outdoor restaurant and now as a growing mini chain, with our sauce featured in nationally distributed prepared food products.

From here the story really takes off, so I'll let the chefs tell the rest of it as they share some of our prize-winning recipes with you. I can only hope you have as much fun and as many good meals as I have enjoyed around the barbecue pit..

ROB SHAWGER
Founding Partner, Pig Beach

SCOVERING BARBECUE

What do you think of when you hear the word "barbecue"? Your reaction is, we'd bet, just what ours still is—you picture a gathering of friends and family, lots of finger lickin' and napkins, icy drinks flowing and mounds of meat at the center of a big ol' table covered with a checkered oilcloth.

No matter how many times we fire up the smoker or join in competition, the camaraderie of the barbecue world is where you'll find our hearts. This is the story of how two guys trained in the world of haute cuisine came together to master this centuries-old craft, with the goal of learning from great pitmasters as we participated in barbecue events around the country.

FROM SHANE: I grew up in the South, and that meant I had to be a college football fan—they just kinda go hand in hand. And once a fan, you become skilled at weekend road trips and chasing down the best barbecue wherever you land. In later years, while I (like Matt) was cheffing at world-famous restaurants, I would travel around the world cooking at food festivals and charity dinners, again always on the lookout for great barbecue, not to mention hunting down the best local cookbook bookstores!

My road map of barbecue started in my hometown of West Palm Beach, Florida. Now, West Palm is not necessarily a barbecue mecca, but there were two local places where I cut my teeth. The foremost was Blue Front Bar-B-Q, a favorite of my grandfather and uncle. Norris Nelson started slingin' "'cue" on Fifteenth and Tamarind Avenue in 1964 and was instantly famous for his thick mustardy house on my days off. Then we decided we were slick enough to begin entering local competitions, and amazingly, we began winning them. That led to a trip to Texas Hill Country to sample the best barbecue the state had to offer. Without Rob's passion exciting me, I'm not sure I would have found a home in the barbecue world. But I am eternally grateful that I have.

It didn't take Rob and me long to figure out that we loved cooking together and that we made a great barbecue duo. We formed our competition team, Salty Rinse Barbecue Team, and made our entry into the World Series of barbecue competition, Memphis in May. In our first try, we won first place in Poultry and second place in Whole Hog. We couldn't believe our luck!

It was time to get really serious! I decided to leave Italian cooking (for the time being, anyway!) and go whole hog (pun intended) into barbecue. Rob found the real estate while I worked on a menu. On a vacant lot in Brooklyn, we built Pig Beach as a summer pop-up barbecue joint. My brother-in-law, the late Jeff Michner, came on board as executive chef to help me create our first menu. The name came from Rob's fishing trips around the Bahamas where there is, in fact, a beach known for the feral pigs that swim in the waters around it. It was an amusing side note that the lot was right next to Brooklyn's notorious Gowanus Canal.

The pop-up was so successful that within a year, we decided it should be a year-round, full-service restaurant. We began our expansion to revamp and build out into the attached building on our lot. With all our excitement and positive momentum, Shane left his highly praised position as the corporate chef of Balthazar to join us as our director of operations, using his years of restaurant experience to help take our operation to the next level, guiding our expansion and product development. We have been so lucky to receive many, many accolades from diners and restaurant critics alike. The amazing thing is that it is still fun to go to work and it is still challenging to enter competitions and win, win, win. And most of all, to continue to learn from the giants of the barbecue circuit and draw more people into that great big family of barbecue.

FROM SHANE AND MATT: Throughout our journey, it has been the barbecue family that has really drawn us all into the core of barbecue life. For more on each member of our family, please see page 282. Coming from the fine-dining world, we treasure the pitmasters who have generously shared with us the skills they learned from past masters, just as we learned from the master chefs who were our mentors in the world of haute cuisine.

As we have traveled across the United States to help so many of these amazing pitmasters with events, dinners, fund-raisers, and general competitions, it has been deeply rewarding to have them cook with us at Pig Beach and at events like Memphis in May. We still look forward to learning something new from each pitmaster every time we cook together. And it is a thrill to take the lessons we learned from the classic culinary world and the foods of our heritage and incorporate them into barbecue traditions. As we welcome you into our barbecue family, we hope to share our enthusiasms so that together, we can expand to one united family of barbecue.

A LITTLE BARBECUE HISTORY

Most of us are more than familiar with the word "barbecue," but we rarely think about the who, why, when, and where of it. It just seems like something that has always been, whether we are talking about a pit barbecue, a backyard get-together, picking up some barbecue, grilling, the meat itself, or the cooking of it.

We would guess—and historians would most likely agree—that barbecue in some form started as soon as fire was discovered. Or maybe even before that, when animals were caught in natural fires and it was discovered that the cooked meat tasted pretty darn good.

Many indigenous peoples the world over still practice a form of early barbecue. Food is still cooked in an earth oven, placed in a pre-dug pit using lava-hot rocks as the heat source. The pit is covered with leaves or wet sacks and dirt to hold the heat for the long cooking period required. Some cultures, such as the Aboriginal peoples of Australia and some tribes of Central Asia, place the food, usually the whole animal or bird, directly in the pit and cover it with dirt only. The Mayan cultures of Mexico still cook in earth ovens, creating the much-loved barbacoa, as do the Māori with their *hāngi*, Hawaiians with the *imu*, and Fijians through the *lovo*. New England clam bakes are still cooked in this ancient fashion.

As the exploration of the Americas unfolded, European explorers discovered open, rather than closed, pit methods of cooking throughout the Caribbean. Throughout the islands, once a fire pit was created, branches of green wood were placed over it to hold whatever was being "barbecued." The green wood was too wet to burn and kept an even base for the cooking food. This method was also practiced by enslaved Africans who, early on, found themselves abandoned by explorers in these new lands. It was also practiced by the Native peoples of North America. When the east coast of North America began to be settled by Europeans, this basic style of cooking was adapted and expanded. As it evolved, the cooks were usually enslaved Africans or, occasionally, Native Americans. Only very rarely was the pitmaster European.

Perhaps once fire was more easily controlled, it just seemed easier and quicker to build a fire and place the meat directly over it. As time passed, methods to control the heat and the distance between the fire and the meat improved drastically. But no matter the method, for generations it remained hot and dirty work. Because of this, cooking with fire has almost always been a task relegated to slave labor or hired help. Since they were also given the less desirable, harder-to-cook pieces left over after the rest of the household had taken the choice bits, cooks made it their job to learn how to make these lesser cuts tastier and even more inviting than the lean cuts their masters coveted.

In America, the early pitmasters of the Southern states were almost always enslaved Africans, who developed great skill working with whole hogs and tougher cuts of meat. Today, pitmasters and food lovers throughout the country acknowledge the skill still held by the progeny of these early barbecue cooks. We, along with many other barbecue lovers, hold the artistry of such esteemed Black pitmasters as Rodney Scott, Moe Cason, and Ed Mitchell in the highest regard.

As we gorged ourselves on the history of barbecue in America, we have had the privilege of meeting and learning from so many Black pitmasters across the country. Unfortunately, because participating in contests is expensive, time-consuming, and labor-intensive, pitmasters from smaller local barbecue pit stops don't always have the opportunity to participate and therefore aren't as well-known as they should be. So if you come upon a barbecue pit anywhere in your travels, don't hesitate to stop in for some 'cue and a chat—you might just taste the smokin'-best mess of ribs or pile of pulled pork you've ever had.

Barbecue is now a familiar word all over the world, but more frequently than not, it translates to "backyard grilling." Although we appreciate a good grill (see pages 130–131), there are still regions in America that define true barbecue. Many of these areas have different styles of barbecue and each one is a source of enormous local pride. Some types of barbecue, like those in the Carolinas and Tennessee, use pork only, while others, such as those in Texas, Missouri, and Kentucky, feature other meats: primarily beef, but also poultry and lamb. Not only are different proteins used, but varying rubs and sauces further define a local style. At Pig Beach, we have absorbed all these styles and feel that this has given us the ability to create our signature barbecue and the flavors of the accompanying seasonings, sauces, and go-withs.

Although most backyard barbecue is cooked on a standard grill, that is not how "real" barbecue is done. What is now known as "classic barbecue" is done in a smoker, an apparatus that can be similar to a grill in looks (and you *can* turn a backyard grill into a smoker if push comes to shove), but instead of cooking meat through direct heat as you do when grilling, it is cooked with smoke through a long, slow process that requires low, closely maintained heat (see pages 33–36). This long, slow process allows the flavor of whatever type of wood is used to create the smoke to gently work its way into the heart of the meat, lending a unique, rich, deep, satisfying, almost indescribable essence to the finished meat.

AMERICAN REGIONAL BARBECUE

The age-old argument of where in America barbecue truly began will probably rage on forever. Whose pig is better than whose cow can start an instant argument. So, we will stick with the basics and let the food literati duke it out in food academia. For our money, there is no better place to start than the sweet **Carolinas**. Here we have friends and family torn between mustard or vinegar, whole hog or pork shoulder. One thing is for sure: the pig reigns supreme in both states, and it is all delicious. Pig rules in North and South Carolina because early explorers left their stock to forage on its own, and to this day you will find feral hogs throughout the Carolina backwoods.

North and South Carolina feature widely different methods of preparation, although they are both known for the beloved "Carolina Q," often thought of as the oldest style of barbecue in America. North Carolina is basically split between eastern and western regions; both use pork and hardwoods indigenous to the state, such as hickory and oak. The major difference is that in the western part of the state, pork shoulder is the meat of choice and a vinegar-and-tomato-based sauce is the chosen lubricant. This style is generally referred to as "Lexington style." There are a great many terrific western Carolina–style barbecue joints, especially in Lexington, North Carolina. One of the standouts is the legendary Lexington Barbecue, locally called "The Monk," dating back to the '60s. Equally spectacular

are Bar-B-Q Center of Lexington and Speedy's Barbecue. A relative newcomer who slightly breaks with tradition is Buxton Hall Barbecue in Asheville, where Elliott Moss and Meherwan Irani are cooking whole hogs and using their chef-trained chops to create a fresh, new style of western North Carolina barbecue. Also, not to be missed is the South Carolina–style barbecue hash and the potently delicious Cheerwine-bourbon slushy.

Eastern North Carolina is whole hog crazy, always slow smoked with hickory or oak in pits. Once cooked, the meat is generally chopped and doused with a tangy vinegar-and-pepper sauce. This is purist 'cue: whole animals with minimal seasonings gently cooked to let their piggy goodness shine through. As the old adage goes, they really do use every part of the pig but the squeal. Just writing about this makes us long for some of the good down-home stuff with a couple slices of squishy white bread and some slaw. A guy who brings this together beyond compare is our friend Sam Jones at his eponymous restaurant in Winterview, North Carolina. Sam is the third generation of the Jones family cooking whole hogs. He started cooking alongside his grandfather Pete Jones and dad, Bruce Jones, at the family restaurant, the Skylight Inn, truly one of America's barbecue gems.

Let's cruise down south to ol' South Carolina, one of Shane's favorite places! Not to bring up rivalries again, but some say barbecue as we now know it started in South Carolina (though there are plenty of folks who say Virginia was its birthplace). Regardless of who's right, there is some amazing barbecue to be found in the Palmetto State. There are thought to be two main styles of barbecue in South Carolina, Pee Dee and Midland, as well as a variety of local styles that might incorporate methods from all over the country. The Pee Dee style, named for the Pee Dee River watershed, is usually based on whole hogs cooked over slow-burning coals in brick or cinder-block pits. The mainstay of this region is its sometimes hot-as-hell vinegar sauce, which can be as simple as vinegar, salt, and a big dose of cayenne pepper. Rodney Scott is the master of this style, without peer! His whole hog mastery at his restaurant, Rodney Scott's Whole Hog BBQ in Charleston, has earned Scott a coveted James Beard award, the highest distinction a chef can get in the United States. Also well worth the drive from Charleston up to Hemingway, South Carolina, is Scott's Bar-B-Que, where Rodney got his start.

On to Midlands-style barbecue. Now we're talking about hardwood-smoked pigs and hams and shoulders with that "Carolina Gold" mustard sauce. This is what makes South Carolina barbecue: mustard with a little touch of brown sugar and vinegar makes that ol' hog sing! One of our favorite spots for this amazing taste thrill is Sweatman's BBQ in Holly Hill. You absolutely cannot watch the University of South Carolina Gamecocks play without stopping by Big T's Bar-B-Que in Columbia, South Carolina. Old-school barbecue at its best, for sure.

Since you're now planning a trip to Charleston to see Rodney and his hogs, let's talk about some of the incredible barbecue happening in the Holy City. First in mind is not what you might think of as traditional South Carolina barbecue at Lewis Barbecue. John Lewis originally started honing his skills in Texas and decided Charleston would be a good place to open his namesake restaurant, and believe us, the town is all the luckier for it. John's Texas-style brisket and his "weekends only" beef ribs are some of the best we've ever eaten. Shane's mom buys John's mac "n" cheese by the quart and keeps her cache all to herself, and his

son, Garrett, has a standing request for John's Hatch chile barbecue sauce as a Christmas gift. Swig & Swine is the home of Anthony DiBernardo and has become a regular on our barbecue rotation. His sausage, pork belly, and wings are stellar. Home Team BBQ's secret weapons are their barbecued chicken skins, killer barbecue tacos, and a tag team of frozen cocktails: the Gamechanger, their signature drink, and frozen Irish coffee, Shane's partner Jenifer's favorite.

Beef is king in **Texas** and brisket is the star. Although there are varying types of barbecue throughout the state, most of us think about the barbecue of Central Texas. Post oak is the wood of choice and the rub is usually just salt and pepper. A tomato-based sauce is often served alongside the barbecue but is generally frowned upon by locals. Most barbecue spots will also offer sausages, pork ribs, pulled pork, and chicken, along with huge beef ribs. No matter what barbecue you order, it will be accompanied by onions, pickles, and a slice of squishy white bread. In West Texas you will find more open grilling, most often featuring goat and lamb. In the southernmost part of the state, you'll find barbacoa, with its deep Spanish influences; the meat, frequently a cow's head, was originally cooked in pits, but is now more often grilled than smoked.

Kansas City, Missouri, offers a variety of barbecued meats and poultry, all with a well-spiced dry rub and a zesty tomato-based sauce served on the side, and interesting side dishes are often the big draw. There is no signature wood, although many prefer the local Missouri white oak. Arthur Bryant's Barbeque, once called the best restaurant in the world by famed journalist and food writer Calvin Trillin, is best known for their introduction of burnt ends to the barbecue world. Now most Kansas City spots serve these tasty tidbits along with a sweet and sticky barbecue sauce. Jones Bar-B-Q has recently come to fame through a feature in a *Queer Eye* television makeover, although their barbecue is noteworthy also. Gates BBQ and Joe's Kansas City Bar-B-Que are a couple of other local favorites.

From our perspective, there are two types of **Tennessee** barbecue: eastern whole hog or shoulder, and Memphis "wet" and "dry" ribs. The whole hogs and shoulders are cooked over hardwoods and generally sauced with a spiced vinegar sauce that seems to have migrated from the Carolinas' sauce playbook. The "dry" rib is a pork sparerib or baby back rib liberally seasoned with salt, pepper, and spices and either slow smoked or hot grilled over charcoal, like is done at the famous Charlie Vergo's Rendezvous. The "wet" Memphis rib is seasoned with a rub and then glazed with a tomato-based barbecue sauce; this style is probably the most common throughout the United States.

There are *soooo* many great places to get barbecue in Tennessee, but of course we've got our favorites. Throughout the years we've been driving to compete at Memphis in May, our usual pit stop has been Nashville, where we spend the night. Our two favorite pitmasters and their spots are Martin's Bar-B-Que Joint, where Pat Martin smokes up some killer whole hogs in his temple to great Tennessee barbecue, and Peg Leg Porker, where Carey Bringle's dry ribs are awesome; you can't miss his Memphis sushi and his namesake Peg Leg bourbon. The latter makes one of Shane's favorite cocktails, the Pork and Stormy.

Memphis is all about ribs, but you can also find some other pretty unique barbecue dishes. Commissary BBQ in Germantown is what some consider to be the birthplace of barbecue nachos, while the Bar-B-Q Shop has its famous barbecued spaghetti, which is perfectly cooked pasta with glistening pulled pork on top. You can also find a mean Texas toast pulled pork sandwich there. Coletta's, a terrific Italian restaurant, is Memphis's oldest, and it just happens to serve one of Elvis's favorites, a barbecued pizza. Also not to be missed are Cozy Corner BBQ and Payne's Bar-B-Que, both classic Memphis hangouts.

A short drive from downtown Memphis in Horn Lake, Mississippi, you will find Memphis BBQ Co. It is helmed by not just one but two of the best pitmasters in the country, both multiple-time champions: our good friend John David Wheeler and Melissa Cookston, the goddess of barbecue. Their restaurant has it all—killer ribs, burgers, sides, and frosty cocktails. Well worth the drive!

And finally, while it's not technically barbecue, there is one more master of pork and smoke that you can't miss: Mr. Allen Benton. Benton's Smoky Mountain Country Hams in Madisonville, Tennessee, has been making "hams of the gods" for years. Shane first fell in love with Benton's products when he was a line cook at Lespinasse, a four-star restaurant in Manhattan. One of the Benton secrets is its smoked ham hocks, which Shane feels are black magic in the kitchen. He always has one in the freezer and suggests you do, too.

Kentucky has so many of a cook's favorite things—bourbon, bluegrass, the Kentucky Derby, and Ale-8-One, that elusive caffeinated ginger ale, a clutch hangover choice. It also has mutton barbecue, slow-smoked sheep cooked over pits fired with local hickory wood. Sheep spareribs are one of the choice cuts. The mutton is usually slow smoked over hickory wood and served with "dip," a Worcestershire-based au jus of sorts. Our two favorites are both in Owensboro, which is ground zero for barbecued mutton: Moonlite Bar-B-Q Inn, which also has a fantastic burgoo and dessert pies to die for, and Old Hickory Bar-B-Q, which has a killer barbecued bologna.

Alabama is home to one of the country's most famous pitmasters, Big Bob Gibson, who was the great-grandfather of the wife of our friend Chris Lilly, another great pitmaster. The signature Alabama barbecue, smoked chicken with Alabama white sauce, can be found at his barbecue spot, Big Bob Gibson Bar-B-Q in Decatur. The mayonnaise-based sauce defines this style, and is also used as a table sauce for other foods. In other parts of the state, you will find pork shoulder and ribs served with a tomato-based sauce.

BARBECUE BASICS

SAM: SIZE ROLL   NEW SPACE-SAVING BOX   36% SMALLER BO

CAUTION: SHARP EDGE   IATENCIONI BORDE AFILADO

BOAR**LK**

18 inches x 500 feet
45.7cm x 152.4m

EXTRA HEAVY DU
ALUMINUM FO

ynds

Pellicule sevice alimentaire

914SC

A WORD ABOUT SMOKERS

There are a number of different types of smokers available for successful traditional barbecue. You can find electric smokers, box smokers, smoker ovens, steel drum smokers, and many types of kettle smokers. The space you have available, the price you are willing to pay, the type of heat you require, and the ease of control and use you're looking for are just some of the things to consider when buying a smoker.

If there is one thing that rings true throughout the barbecue world, it's that every pitmaster or even weekend cook thinks the smoker they are using is absolutely the best one. Each type has its defenders and its own list of pros and cons to consider. When Shane was buying his first smoker, he found tons of message boards with endless online lists of which manufacturer was making the best cookers on the market. On his first trip to Memphis in May, he says it was like strolling through one of the massive exotic-car dealerships on Manhattan's West Side; Jedmasters, Jambo pits, and Klose pits were the equivalent of Ferraris, Lamborghinis, and Porsches in Memphis!

In the professional kitchens we grew up in, the type of stove the restaurant had was all part of the learning experience. When you cook on a fabulously expensive streamlined French Bonnet stove for the first time, you just know you've hit the big leagues. As pitmasters, we feel the same about smokers! Everyone needs to start on an inexpensive kettle grill or barrel smoker to learn how to control heat and flame-ups and ultimately produce that sweet clean smoke you need to make delicious barbecue. This also gives the cook the time to figure out what wood or charcoal best suits their style. But as with most things in life, you get what you pay for. This is especially true with kitchen and cooking equipment. Gauge of steel, how well it's welded, double-walled firebox—these are all key concepts to learn if you're going to keep that fire slow and steady for long periods of time.

At Pig Beach, we use an Ole Hickory Pits wood smoker, which has a convection system to keep the heat moving throughout the smoking process. This is the smoker most often used in major commercial and contest settings, as it requires less wood than other smokers and its continuous circulation of heat and smoke cooks evenly and consistently. It is powered by a thermostatically controlled burner, which fires up the wood and reignites it whenever the internal temperature drops lower than desired. It is easy to clean and movable. These smokers are very expensive, however, and not for the occasional backyard use.

Among the types of smokers we recommend are:

OFFSET SMOKER: Also called a stick burner, horizontal offset smoker, or just an "offset," this is a two-section cooker usually set on wheels so that it can be moved easily. This was actually the first type of smoker that Shane had—a good old Lang reverse-flow smoker proudly made in Georgia. We've driven it all over the USA doing competitions and exhibitions, and it remains so easy to cook with that we'd be hard-pressed to recommend any other. Actually, that old gal is still being used by Ribdiculous team member Damon Wise, who has hauled it all over the New York metropolitan area doing barbecue pop-ups for takeout. This is certainly a testament to its durability.

Matt and Rob began with a similar offset smoker from Tucker Barbecues. This was the first pit Matt was exposed to that wasn't a Weber kettle. He was quickly enthralled with its grandiose size and look.

An offset smoker is normally composed of an extended horizontal metal enclosure or box called the cooking chamber, with an interior grill plate to hold the meat, and separate firebox, in which heat and smoke are created, attached to one end of the cooking chamber. The cooking chamber has a small hatchlike opening or a smokestack (sometimes both) from which excess smoke can be let out. The firebox has an access door as well as a vent. When the fire is lit, the smoke travels through the cooking chamber, where it cooks and flavors the meat as it makes its way outward through the hatch or smokestack. The level of heat and smoke is adjusted by maneuvering the vents. An advantage to this style of smoker is that the firebox can be refilled throughout the cooking process without opening the cooking chamber. However, meat cooked in this fashion is generally rotated frequently to allow for even cooking, as the meat nearest the firebox will get more smoke and heat than that at the other end. This is the style preferred by some grill masters, who feel that it imparts the most authentic barbecue-smoke taste.

There are tons of stick burners out there, readily available at your local big box hardware store. A couple of brands we have used and liked are Yoder and Meadow Creek, which we recommend for those just starting out. Lang remains close to our hearts. David Klose makes some pretty amazing custom pits, but our dream would be a Jambo pit all dolled up in shiny paint! Tuffy Stone has one of the coolest ones we've ever seen, and we covet it.

VERTICAL WATER SMOKER: This is the most commonly owned backyard smoker. It is easy to use and maintain and requires only a small amount of space to operate. The most common is the Weber Smokey Mountain cooker, but there are many options ranging from electric to full-blown big competition rigs. It is an upright domed container that comprises three sections: The bottom section is the firebox, where charcoal and wood chips generate heat and smoke. The middle compartment holds the water pan; once the water is hot, it helps keep the meat moist as well as evenly dispersing heat. The top compartment, which takes up almost half the smoker, from the water pan up to the domed lid, is where the smoking occurs. The grate for the meat is usually placed in the center of the top compartment.

Shane has had a few electric vertical smokers in his restaurant kitchens, where he's used them to get some smoke flavor on meats. At Craftsteak, a gently modified Bradley electric smoker allowed the cooks to use wood chunks rather than the sawdust pucks they sell for this purpose with pretty darn good results. Unfortunately, that poor fella couldn't handle working in a professional kitchen and had a meltdown latterly. Shane then got a Cookshack electric smoker, which gave the cooks more versatility. He was teased incessantly by the late great food writer Josh Ozersky, who said that no matter what Shane put in that box, it couldn't be called barbecue. No matter Josh's opinion, the smoked meats, fish, cheeses, foie gras, and vegetables that came out of it tasted pretty damn good.

As Matt and Rob continued into the smoked-meat world, they upgraded from their offset smoker to a vertical smoker by Pitmaker called the BBQ Vault, an incredible unit made in Humble, Texas. This smoker holds its heat incredibly well and is perfect for ribs, briskets, chicken, and pork butts.

We guess that our favorite vertical smoker is the Fatboy Backwoods Smoker from Dixie, Louisiana. It is extremely easy to use, very consistent in outcome, and exceedingly durable, making it a big favorite on the barbecue competition circuit. An honorable mention has to go to our friend Mark Lambert and his Sweet Swine O'Mine Little Red Smoker. We cooked on a couple of them for a fun contest sponsored by Operation BBQ Relief at the US Coast Guard station on Staten Island. They are big enough to feed several people, fun to cook on, and so darn cute.

KETTLE SMOKER: These range from the expensive ceramic Kamado Joe classic from Japan to the everyday Weber backyard kettle grill, which can be converted into a smoker. There are also stovetop kettle smokers that make amazingly tasty smoked food on a kitchen stovetop.

We still love cooking on a Weber kettle grill. When you live in the city with just a pinch of a backyard, this workhorse can be your go-to all summer long. Super easy to use, low-maintenance, and very versatile says it all! You can grill a terrific steak, cook a whole chicken beer can style, or go slow and low for some killer baby back ribs. A little bit of practice is what gives good results. We like to use a combination of hardwood charcoal and wood chunks when cooking on a Weber, for both flavor and maximum heat for searing power. Another type of grill we like is the Kudu grill. It is more of an open-fire grill, with two levels of cooking surfaces and a large skillet option as well.

Ceramic kettle smokers control smoke through airflow. A ceramic insert sits between the fire and the grill and forces the heat out around the edges of the kettle, away from the meat. People always ask us about ceramic kettle smokers like the Big Green Egg and Kamado Joe. They are both a great introduction to low-and-slow barbecue and hot-and-fast grilling, and they do both incredibly well. They are extremely well insulated and maintain even heat when they are used for long periods of time. The only drawback is that neither of these is quite large enough to do the job if you want to cook low and slow to feed a crowd. That being said, there is no better hot-and-fast grill than one of these styles. Plus, with a little practice (again, that word!), you can make incredible pizza in one of these kettle grills.

As we mentioned earlier, our first trip to Memphis in May was a droolfest of amazing firepower. Like most things in life, there's a top shelf to strive for. One of our mentors, John Markus, has a nonpareil collection of smokers, so we asked him what smoker he thought was the best in the world. His answer: "When I first met Chris Lilly on South Beach, he was cooking on his Jedmaster rig, and it was love at first sight." The Jedmaster, completely overbuilt and incredibly efficient, is now the most highly sought-after smoker. Difficult to find and extraordinarily expensive, we covet one, too!

CREATING YOUR OWN SMOKER USING AN INEXPENSIVE KETTLE GRILL: Prepare the fire as usual across the bottom base of the kettle. When the coals are hot, move them to one side of the base. Place one or two metal pans filled with water opposite the coals in the base, then place a couple of handfuls of wood chips on the hot coals. Lay the grate into place. If the grate is hinged, place the hinged section over the coals. Place the meat on the grate over the water pans. Cover, placing the vent in the cover directly over the meat. Close all the vents. You will have to watch the smoker constantly to ensure that it is smoking and to make certain that the temperature stays around 225°F. If it goes above that, take off the lid and let the coats burn off some; if it goes below 225°F, add more coals. You will need to add fresh soaked wood chips throughout the cooking time, usually about every 90 minutes or so. The cooking time will depend on the type of protein you are smoking; fish will usually take less than an hour, while large pieces of meat can take up to 8 hours.

Buying a smoker:

1 Price is usually the first consideration. Smokers range from around $100 to many, many thousands of dollars. We suggest starting with a less expensive one and moving up to a more costly one if you decide that weekly barbecuing is in your future.

2 After price, the capacity of the smoker is important. If you are going to smoke small pieces of meat, a chicken, or just a couple of racks of ribs, a small smoker will do the trick. If you have a big family, love to entertain, or plan on catering local events, then look for a smoker that has the capacity to smoke for a crowd.

3 Ease of operation can determine how often you use the smoker. You want to be able to easily manage the temperature controls, cleaning, and maintenance, and make sure a drip pan is part of the operation. Some smokers can also be used as grills. If this is a benefit you require, make sure the smoker you choose is multipurpose.

4 If you have unlimited outdoor space, the size of the smoker will not be important, but if you don't, you need to be clear about how much room you need for the smoker to function efficiently. Not only will you need room for the smoker itself, you'll need to place it away from buildings, leaving space to walk around it and to allow for proper airflow.

Direct flow Horizon smoker

The wood smoke does two things to the meat: it seasons, and it adds a desired inviting burnished reddish-brown color to the finished dish. And yet you don't want either of these attributes to overpower the meat itself. Too much or too little smoke works in much the same way as too much or too little salt—either one is detrimental to the final flavor. Every pitmaster has a preferred wood, and each type of wood has its place. Just remember that it is totally about building and developing the perfect balance of flavor.

There are many different woods that can help you achieve your signature smoke. All the fruit woods—cherry, apple, peach, and pear—are on the mild, sweet side. They are most often used in combination with more intense woods or as the primary wood for smoking milder foods such as chicken, turkey breast, or fish.

In the medium range of smoke production, you will find birch, maple, hickory, oak, and pecan woods. Any of these can be used to smoke beef or game, including wild birds. Traditionally, hickory is most often used to smoke pork.

The He-Man of smoke production is mesquite, normally used in the southwest and in Texas, where it is grown. It is always used for barbacoa, often in combination with a lighter wood. Those who love its flavor generally only use it for a defined amount of time early in the smoking so it doesn't overpower the meat.

If you want to add just a touch of smoke when grilling, you can use a small amount of wood chips from any of the abovementioned woods on top of whatever you are using to create heat.

No matter the wood you choose, it is most important that it be dry or cured. Green or wet wood, as well as resinous woods like pine, will emit creosote, which will render your finished food inedible. Dry woods for smoking or grilling can usually be found at big box stores, neighborhood hardware stores, and (always) online. Wood chunks and logs burn slower and longer than thin pieces and are recommended to create the long, slow smoke you desire. Chips and sawdust burn too hot and too fast and will result in a harsh, acrid taste. The most important point to remember is that you never want the smoke to overpower the meat. Temperature zones of 200° to 275°F, depending on what you are cooking, will keep the smoke under control.

At Pig Beach we use cherry wood for smoking ribs, sausages, turkey, wings, and tri-tip steaks; hickory for pork butts; and a combination of hickory and cherry for our renowned brisket.

THE STALL AND THE TEXAS CRUTCH

"The stall" is a temperature range, about 155° to 160°F, where the rate of evaporation cools the meat faster than the meat can cook, causing its internal temperature to "stall." There are a few different philosophies on how to manage this.

To prevent the stall, some pit masters like to "wrap," which is literally wrapping the protein in foil to trap the heat inside. This is known as the "Texas crutch." Others like to increase the temperature of their cooker, which will cause the meat to push through the stall. Some pitmasters find a happy medium by wrapping the meat in butcher paper at the stall. The paper locks in heat but, since it is porous, allows some moisture to escape.

The point is, you have many options at the stall. We encourage you to play around to find what works best for you. Just don't be afraid to fail.

SMOKE RING

In barbecue talk, a smoke ring is not that wafting circle of tobacco smoke that sophisticated ladies in the '40s blew between sips of a cocktail. In this case, it refers to the pale pink ring just under the exterior layer of a piece of smoked meat. Usually about ¼ inch thick, is most often found on solid pieces of meat such as brisket, but can also be found on other cuts. A smoke ring indicates a perfectly smoked product, but if a smoke ring is not present, it does not necessarily mean the meat is not going to be well flavored.

The smoke ring is a natural result of nitrous oxide in the burning wood. Green wood produces a lot of smoke, but it also produces creosote, which you do not want under any circumstances. Wood should be dry, with some bark attached, as the bark produces the nitrous oxide that creates the ring.

There are a number of other tricks to ensure that your product has the desired ring. Meat absorbs smoke best when its surface is wet, whether from a marinade, a mop, or a spritz of moisture added during the smoking process. If your meat has a thick fat cap, that will make it difficult for the smoke to penetrate, so trim it down some, leaving enough fat to add moisture and flavor during smoking. If you are using a dry rub, do not coat the meat with a thick layer of the rub or it will block smoke penetration. Above all else, long, slow, low-heat, temperature-controlled smoking will ensure a perfect smoke ring as well as perfectly flavored meat. To win any barbecue competition, you will need both of these to capture the judges' votes.

LONG SMOKING

Smoking long and slow renders perfectly moist, tender finished meat or fish. Smoking over an extra-long period of time, such as with Italian salumi, can also be used to remove all the moisture from a protein, leaving behind a dry, acidic coating and resulting in a dry, bacteria-free finished product.

TOOLS AND TOYS FOR BARBECUING AND GRILLING

DISPOSABLE ALUMINUM PANS are a pitmaster's best friend. They are portable, recyclable, and the perfect large container to both season and cook in! They come in especially handy when cooking outside or at an off-site competition. The most common brand is probably Reynolds, but we use whatever sturdy aluminum pans we can purchase in bulk at the best possible price. Large roasting-size pans are perfect for seasoning large pieces of meat, such as ribs, brisket, and pork butts, while mid-size pans are terrific for turkey breast and chicken.

ALUMINUM FOIL is another crucial tool for smoking meats. It has so many uses, many of which relate to easy cleanup. We often use it to wrap tables when seasoning large amounts of meat to give us an easily disposable work surface. Of course, it is also used to wrap proteins for the famous "Texas crutch" (see page 35). We are never without it, in the restaurant or on the road. Brand isn't as important as type; we strongly recommend using heavy-duty or extra-heavy-duty aluminum foil. It is stronger through the smoking process and prevents those nasty little cuts or

PIG BEACH POULTRY SEASONING

It isn't uncommon for pitmasters to develop a signature "Famous Rub" by blending a selection of their favorite rubs together. For this seasoning, we did just that! When we started developing recipes for the restaurant, we were using our All-Purpose Barbecue Seasoning (page 44) for everything. The poultry items—wings and such—were GREAT, but we wanted something to give them extra oomph. We began with our all-purpose seasoning and then added to it to create this recipe.

MAKES ABOUT ½ CUP

Combine the seasoning with the rub and sugar in a small bowl and stir to blend completely.

Transfer to a food-safe container, cover, and store in a cool, dark spot for up to 1 month.

¼ cup All-Purpose Barbecue Seasoning (page 44)

¼ cup Tri-Tip Rub (page 48)

1 tablespoon light brown sugar

PRE-SEASONING RUB

We use this mix as a seasoning agent on just about anything we cook. We feel that it is the best ratio of salt to pepper and then the Ac'cent kicks in with the perfect hint of umami that makes everything taste better. Used as a pre-seasoning, it has enormous impact on the finished dish. You can use it just as you would salt and pepper.

MAKES 1 CUP

Combine the salt, pepper, and Ac'cent in a small food-safe container. Cover and shake to combine.

Store at room temperature for up to 3 months.

½ cup kosher salt

¼ cup ground black pepper

1 tablespoon Ac'cent flavor enhancer

PIG BEACH WET RUB

This rub is amazing to use on any steak to really fortify it and build an umami bomb of beefy flavor. You can, when using it on other proteins, substitute the beef base for an appropriate base to match your protein. For example, the substituting pork base makes a terrific rub for a smoked pork loin. Chicken base will do the same for a whole smoked chicken. Use vegetable and mushroom bases to add a wallop of flavor when grilling or smoking vegetables.

MAKES ABOUT ½ CUP

½ cup yellow mustard

¼ cup Better Than Bouillon roasted beef base (see BBQ Bits & Pieces)

2 tablespoons light brown sugar

2 tablespoons honey

2 tablespoons butcher's grind black pepper

1 tablespoon chopped fresh rosemary

2 teaspoons chile flakes

2 teaspoons water

Combine the mustard, beef base, sugar, and honey in a small bowl and stir to blend thoroughly. Add the pepper, rosemary, chile flakes, and water and beat until a paste forms.

Transfer to a food-safe container, cover, and store in the refrigerator for up to 1 month.

BBQ BITS & PIECES: Better Than Bouillon roasted beef base (and other flavors, such as chicken and vegetable) is available from most supermarkets, specialty food stores, and online.

CHIPOTLE BARBECUE RUB

We use this rub on our beer can chicken (page 92), but you can use it on just about anything you like. Just remember, chipotle chiles are simply smoked jalapeños, so they do retain a bit of heat and a lot of smoke!

MAKES ABOUT 1½ CUPS

Combine the sugar, chile powder, paprika, mustard powder, cumin, salt, garlic, onion, and pepper in a medium food-safe container with a lid. Cover and shake well to blend completely.

Store at room temperature for up to 3 months.

½ cup sugar

¼ cup chipotle chile powder

2 tablespoons sweet paprika

1 tablespoon yellow mustard powder

1 tablespoon ground cumin

1 tablespoon kosher salt

1 tablespoon granulated garlic

2 teaspoons granulated onion

1 teaspoon ground black pepper

BRISKET RUB

We use this only when smoking brisket, but that shouldn't keep you from using it on other red meats—maybe even lamb chops or a steak on the backyard grill.

MAKES 2 CUPS

Combine the salt, pepper, garlic, and onion in a food-safe container with a lid. Cover and shake to combine.

Store at room temperature until ready to use, up to 6 months.

¾ cup coarse salt

¾ cup butcher's grind black pepper

1 tablespoon granulated garlic

1 tablespoon granulated onion

TRI-TIP RUB

This is a very simple rub that we use on our smoked and grilled tri-tip steak. It would work equally well on any steak, cooked on the grill or on the stovetop. The sweet paprika adds an indescribable flavor that keeps diners guessing.

MAKES 1 CUP

⅓ cup ground black pepper

⅓ cup granulated garlic

⅓ cup sweet paprika

1 teaspoon ground dried rosemary

Combine the pepper, garlic, paprika, and rosemary in a small bowl and stir to blend well.

Transfer to a food-safe container, cover, and store at room temperature for up to 1 month.

FRIED CHICKEN DREDGE

You can use this flour mixture to make the best fried chicken you've ever had, OR you can use it to dredge other meats or fish when you want something more than just flour, salt, and pepper. We use it on our sticky ribs (page 126).

MAKES ABOUT 4½ CUPS

4 cups all-purpose flour

3 tablespoons cornstarch

2 tablespoons granulated garlic

2 tablespoons granulated onion

1 tablespoon kosher salt

1 tablespoon ground black pepper

1 tablespoon dried oregano

2 teaspoons Old Bay seasoning

1 teaspoon cayenne pepper

Combine the flour and cornstarch in a large bowl. Add the garlic, onion, salt, black pepper, oregano, Old Bay, and cayenne. Stir to blend completely.

Transfer to a large food-safe container, cover, and store in a cool, dark spot for up to 3 months.

WORLD CHAMPION CLASSIC BARBECUE SAUCE

This sauce won first place in the tomato-based sauce category at Memphis in May in 2019 (see BBQ Bits & Pieces). It is an original recipe from Shane's team, Ribdiculous, that was passed on to us when we opened Pig Beach. At the restaurant we called it Red Table Sauce, or sometimes Balsamic Barbecue Sauce, but now it is simply our world champion sauce.

MAKES 4 CUPS

1¼ cups ketchup

¾ cup apple juice

¾ cup light corn syrup

½ cup tomato paste

½ cup pure maple syrup

½ cup balsamic vinegar

¼ cup honey

3 tablespoons molasses

2 tablespoons tamari

2 tablespoons Worcestershire sauce

1 tablespoon kosher salt

2 teaspoons ground black pepper

1 teaspoon granulated onion

1 teaspoon granulated garlic

½ teaspoon yellow mustard powder

½ teaspoon cayenne pepper

⅛ teaspoon celery seed

⅛ teaspoon ground cumin

Combine all the ingredients in a medium saucepan and stir to blend completely. Bring to a simmer over medium-low heat, then reduce the heat to maintain a bare simmer and cook, stirring frequently, for about 30 minutes or until the sauce is thick and the flavors have blended. Use a rubber spatula to scrape the bottom of the pan from time to time, as the sugar in the sauce may cause it to stick and burn. Remove from the heat and set aside to cool.

Use immediately or transfer to a nonreactive, food-safe container, cover, and store in the refrigerator for up to 3 months.

BBQ BITS & PIECES: When both of our teams, Ribdiculous and Salty Rinse, were going to Memphis in May in 2019, one of our team chefs, Stephen Fugate, made a big batch of this sauce to split between the teams. Ribdiculous kept their original, and Matt made a few very minor tweaks to the Salty Rinse batch, but essentially each batch tasted about the same. The teams submitted their versions of the sauce to the judges. Ribdiculous was called to the stage as the first-place winner, while Salty Rinse finished something like forty-second! That's Memphis in May for you. No matter whose team took home the prize, this is the sauce that caught the attention of Hormel Foods, resulting the amazing collaboration we have with them today.

WORLD CHAMPION MUSTARD SAUCE

Growing up in Florida, Shane's love of barbecue was sealed by a local mustard-based sauce. This one, based on his childhood favorite, took first place at Memphis in May (see BBQ Bits & Pieces). It is simple to make and keeps for a long time, so it is a great sauce to always have on hand.

MAKES 3 CUPS

Combine the mustard, ketchup, honey, and brown sugar in a medium bowl. Whisk in the hot sauce, followed by the barbecue seasoning, Old Bay, celery seed, and cumin. Whisk to blend completely.

Use immediately or place in a food-safe container, cover, and store in the refrigerator for up to 1 month.

1 cup yellow mustard

½ cup ketchup

½ cup honey

½ cup light brown sugar

¼ cup Frank's RedHot hot sauce

1 tablespoon All-Purpose Barbecue Seasoning (page 44)

1 teaspoon Old Bay seasoning

⅛ teaspoon ground celery seed

⅛ teaspoon ground cumin

BBQ BITS & PIECES: The story behind this sauce is a fun one! It was first created when Pig Beach was merely a pop-up in a broken-down parking lot on a Superfund site. Just before we opened for service, Shane brought in his favorite childhood sauce. He quickly whisked in some yellow mustard and said, "Here you go, Carolina-style mustard barbecue sauce." Matt was blown away by its simplicity, and as he was still learning about the different types of barbecue, he loved this new (to him) flavor. We took that base recipe as an inspiration and created a Pig Beach version. Later on, Matt was watching the smoker one day and got some ideas about refining the sauce. He added his flavors and took it to Memphis in May, where the Salty Rinse team entered it in the mustard sauce competition. On the day of judging, a tornado warning was issued and we all hightailed it back to the hotel. We were sitting around the lobby, drinking and chatting and, of course, waiting to hear the winners. The Salty Rinse team was sure they had lost the prize, but lo and behold, the message came through that the team had won first place. Leaping from a childhood favorite to a chef-refined recipe, our World Champion Mustard Sauce is now in grocery stores all across the country!

ROB'S RIGHTEOUS RED BARBECUE SAUCE

This is one of our prize-winning sauces developed by our partner, Rob Shawger. It is his pride and joy and one of our most successful sauces. It keeps for quite a long time when refrigerated, so it is a good all-purpose sauce to keep on hand for your entire barbecue season.

MAKES 2½ CUPS

1 cup ketchup

¾ cup light brown sugar

¼ cup Heinz chili sauce

¼ cup honey

2 tablespoons Worcestershire sauce

1 tablespoon All-Purpose Barbecue Seasoning (page 44)

2 teaspoons Frank's Red-Hot hot sauce

1½ teaspoons tamari

1½ teaspoons ground black pepper

1 teaspoon kosher salt

1 teaspoon ground oregano

¾ teaspoon Rob's Secret Spice Blend (page 53)

½ teaspoon onion powder

½ teaspoon garlic powder

¼ teaspoon cayenne pepper

Combine the ketchup, sugar, chili sauce, honey, and Worcestershire in a medium saucepan over medium-low heat. Add the barbecue seasoning, hot sauce, tamari, black pepper, salt, oregano, spice blend, onion powder, garlic powder, and cayenne and cook, stirring occasionally, for about 5 minutes or until the sauce begins to simmer. Remove from the heat and set aside to cool.

Use immediately or transfer to a food-safe container, cover, and store in the refrigerator for up to 3 months.

ROB'S SECRET SPICE BLEND

MAKES ½ CUP

Combine the paprika and chile powder in a small bowl. Stir in the coriander, turmeric, cumin, allspice, pepper, salt, fenugreek, ginger, cardamom, cinnamon, nutmeg, and cloves. Stir to blend well.

Transfer to a glass jar with a lid. Cover and store in a cool, dark spot for up to 3 months.

3 tablespoons sweet paprika

1 tablespoon Hatch red chile powder (see page 42)

1 teaspoon ground coriander

1 teaspoon ground turmeric

1 teaspoon ground cumin

1 teaspoon ground allspice

1 teaspoon ground black pepper

1 teaspoon kosher salt

½ teaspoon ground fenugreek

½ teaspoon ground ginger

¼ teaspoon ground green cardamom

¼ teaspoon ground cinnamon

¼ teaspoon ground nutmeg

¼ teaspoon ground cloves

BBQ BITS & PIECES: Rob's Secret Spice Blend was inspired by an Ethiopian blend called berbere. It was a seasoning Matt was using at Del Posto that Rob had loved. On a barbecue Sunday at the beach, Matt brought Rob some berbere to put in his pantry. Later in the summer and with a few vinos under his belt, Rob was in the kitchen making what he said would be his "signature sauce." We watched as he began mixing in all the classic ingredients. He wasn't quite satisfied and then he remembered his container of berbere. He added some to his sauce, LOVED the flavor, and Rob's Righteous Red was born. There is no berbere spice in the final recipe, and there is an even better story about why. Deciphering the recipe that Rob sent, asking Matt to re-create his pourable magic is a whole other story we'll save for another time.

BARBECUE BUFFALO WING SAUCE

The wings at Pig Beach are one of the most popular items on the menu, and we think the sauce has a lot to do with that. The mix of the tangy sauce and heat really hits the flavor spot. Pig Beach wings have been featured on the *Today* show, Food Network's *The Kitchen*, as well as many Instagram feeds around the globe.

MAKES 1 CUP

Combine the barbecue sauce and hot sauce in a small bowl. Whisk in the melted butter.

Use immediately or transfer to a food-safe container, cover, and store in the refrigerator for up to 1 week. Reheat before serving.

½ cup Tangy Hatch Vinegar Barbecue Sauce (page 57)

¼ cup Frank's RedHot hot sauce

4 tablespoons (½ stick) unsalted butter, melted

BBQ BITS & PIECES: Matt is from upstate New York, and for sure, Buffalo wings are a staple in his life. Every Monday night was cheap 10-cent wing night at a local spot. It was a favorite of teenagers because they could eat their weight in wings and catch up on all the high school gossip. When developing the menu for Pig Beach, Matt insisted that we pay homage to his roots with some type of Buffalo wing. This sauce did the trick, with the tanginess, heat, and sweet butter combining to make an incredible explosion of flavors.

CHIMICHURRI SAUCE

Chimichurri is a lively condiment with origins in Argentina, where grilled and smoked meats reign supreme. The base is always a mix of herbs with some acidity from citrus and/or vinegar. It should be rather loose so the cool sauce can be spooned over sizzling-hot meat.

MAKES 1 CUP

¼ cup chopped fresh flat-leaf parsley

2 tablespoons chopped fresh mint

2 tablespoons finely minced shallot

3 garlic cloves, minced

1½ teaspoons chile flakes

1 teaspoon dried oregano

Zest of 1 lemon

¼ cup olive oil

2 tablespoons red wine vinegar

1½ table-spoons fresh lemon juice

1½ teaspoons kosher salt

1½ teaspoons ground black pepper

Combine the parsley, mint, shallot, garlic, chile flakes, and oregano in a small bowl. Add the lemon zest, oil, vinegar, and lemon juice and stir to blend thoroughly. Season with the salt and pepper.

Cover and refrigerate for at least 8 hours to allow the flavors to blend before serving.

STANDARD BRINE

This brine is the perfect way to give your proteins that extra bump up of moisture, texture, and flavor (see BBQ Bits & Pieces). You can brine poultry, meat (particularly pork), and even seafood in whatever container you have that will allow it to be totally covered. We love to use giant (2-gallon) resealable plastic bags. They are convenient and easy to use, and they keep the protein well insulated.

MAKES 1 GALLON

Fill a large container with the water. Add the salt and sugar and stir to help them dissolve. Let the mix sit for about 15 minutes and then stir again. You want to agitate the mixture a bit to dissolve the granules. The brine will look cloudy at the beginning, but as the salt and sugar dissolve and the brine sits, it will become clear. Once clear, the brine is ready to be used.

1 gallon cold water

2 cups kosher salt

2 cups sugar

BBQ BITS & PIECES: To get a little nerdy . . . When you brine a protein, the salt in the brine will begin to draw the moisture out of the meat. The meat does not like having its moisture removed, so since it's in a salted solution, the meat sucks the liquid back in through the process of osmosis, the diffusion of water through a semipermeable membrane, or the meat's cells. Through diffusion, the salt and water within the meat's cells wants to balance itself with the salt and water in the surrounding brine, so the meat will pull more salt and moisture into its cells, resulting in a juicier, beautifully seasoned interior.

CORE
BARBECUE

SALT-AND-PEPPER BRISKET

A whole beef brisket is cut from under the first five ribs of the breast of the cow. It is composed of two muscle segments: the point (also known as the deckle) and the flat. The point is the more flavorful section that many refer to as the "fatty brisket" or "moist brisket," and the flat, having minimal fat, is the "lean brisket." Because it is composed of an enormous amount of connective tissue, brisket is the perfect meat to respond to the long, slow cooking required in smoking.

Brisket smoking is the heaviest time commitment in all of barbecue, other than cooking a whole hog. It requires either a super early morning or an overnight cook to have it ready for dinnertime, so before you start your brisket journey, we feel it is very important to have some good beverages, company, snacks, reading material, or your favorite Netflix series on your phone right at hand.

SERVES 10 TO 12

1 (13- to 15-pound) whole beef brisket

½ cup Pre-Seasoning Rub (page 45)

1 cup yellow mustard

3 cups café grind black pepper (see BBQ Bits & Pieces)

Pat the brisket dry using a clean kitchen towel. Do not use paper towel, as it will disintegrate and stick to the meat.

Using a sharp knife, cut a long, thin line straight down the fattier side of the meat, cutting through the fat layer so you can see where the meat begins. Carefully trim off the fat, leaving about ¼ inch covering the meat. Take care that you do not cut too deeply, exposing the meat. (The first cut is done so you can see where the fat meets the meat and accurately trim the fat down to ¼ inch. If you omit this step, you will be cutting blind and could potentially cut off too much fat and have an exposed "bald spot" on the meat, which will result in a patch of dry brisket.)

Using your knife, carefully remove and discard the "wedge cut," the pocket of fat between the point and the flat. This removes excess fat that will not render during cooking and helps the brisket cook more evenly.

Turn the brisket over so that the fatty side is on the bottom and, holding your knife at an angle, remove and discard the large overhang of hard fat.

Season the entire brisket with the rub and set aside to rest for 30 minutes.

Generously coat the entire brisket with the mustard. Yellow mustard is a terrific flavor enhancer and helps in the development of the bark. Cover the mustard with the pepper and set aside to marinate for 30 minutes. The mustard will help the pepper stick to the brisket during smoking.

While the brisket is marinating, using oak or hickory wood, preheat your smoker to 275°F. Place a heatproof bowl of water close to the heat source. The water acts as a heat diffuser and adds moisture to the smoker chamber, resulting in a juicer final product.

Place a thermometer probe in the thickest part of the brisket's point and place the brisket in the smoker fat-side up. Smoke for 4 to 5 hours or until the internal temperature reaches the stall at 155°F (see page 35), spritzing with the brisket spritz every 30 minutes after the first hour of smoking.

Remove the brisket from the smoker, take out the probe, and wrap the entire brisket in butcher paper. Place the probe back in the meat and return the meat to the smoker. Cook for an additional 6 to 8 hours or until the internal temperature reaches between 195° and 200°F. Remove the brisket from the smoker and set aside in a warm spot to rest for 1 hour or until the internal temperature drops to 155°F. This resting period is very important; if you cut into the brisket while it's too hot instead of letting it rest, it will immediately dry out. We like to say, "Patience, young grasshopper . . . you already waited 12 to 14 hours . . . what's one more?"

When the brisket has rested and you are ready to serve, unwrap and cut, against the grain (see page 136), into slices.

BBQ BITS & PIECES: We like wrapping our brisket in butcher paper at the stall, as we feel it offers the best option for getting through the stall without washing off all the "black gold," also known as the bark.

Café grind black pepper (16 to 18 mesh) is available online and from some specialty food stores. The mesh size (see page 38) is the size of the grind; the higher the number, the finer the grind.

If you want an extra-flavorful mix for your seasoning, do half black pepper and half Butcher's Secret Seasoning (page 42).

CORE BARBECUE

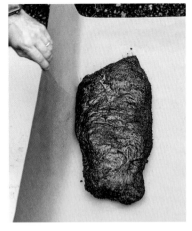
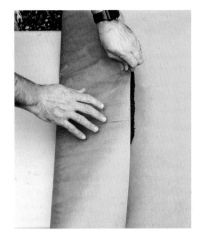
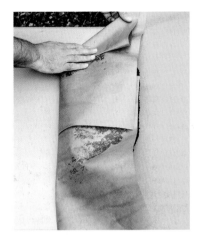
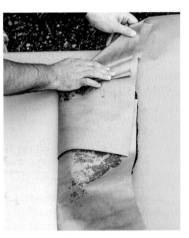
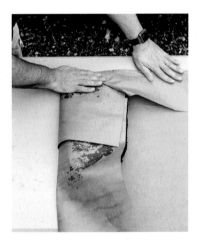

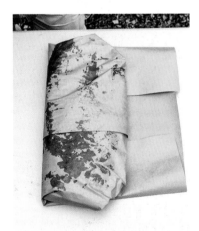

PORK SHOULDER, AKA PULLED PORK

Pulled pork is just about everyone's favorite barbecue meat. Because it is such an economical cut of meat, a pork shoulder is a great starting point to begin pitmaster training, as it won't hurt your wallet too much if your first try doesn't work as well as you hope.

There is nothing better than a slightly sweet roll piled high with pulled pork and some tangy barbecue sauce dripping off the sides. You can, of course, have your own take on a pulled pork sandwich—maybe some coleslaw, some pickles, some hot sauce—just make it your own!

SERVES 8 TO 10

1 (8- to 10-pound) bone-in pork shoulder

½ cup Pre-Seasoning Rub (page 45)

2 cups All-Purpose Barbecue Seasoning (page 44), plus more for sprinkling

3 cups All-Purpose Barbecue Spritz (page 68)

4 cups Tangy Hatch Vinegar Barbecue Sauce (page 57)

Pat the pork shoulder dry using a clean kitchen towel. Do not use paper towel, as it will disintegrate and stick to the meat.

Season the entire shoulder with the rub and set aside to rest for 30 minutes. The meat will begin to sweat as the salt in the rub draws out moisture. This will help the seasoning stick to the meat.

Using 1 cup of the barbecue seasoning, generously coat the entire shoulder. Set aside to marinate for an additional 30 minutes.

While the shoulder is marinating, using hickory wood, preheat your smoker to 250°F.

Place a thermometer probe in the center of the shoulder and place the shoulder in the smoker, away from the heat source. Smoke for 1 hour, then begin spritzing with barbecue spritz every 30 minutes for the next 4 hours or until the internal temperature reaches 155°F. This is the point at which the rate of evaporation of the moisture in the meat will cool off the shoulder, preventing the temperature from rising.

Now is the time to apply the "Texas crutch" where the shoulder gets wrapped. At Pig Beach, we love wrapping it in plastic wrap and foil (see BBQ Bits & Pieces) as it acts as a "poor folks' sous vide," locking in all the juices and heat as the wrap helps the meat push through the stall (see page 35). When

ooo continued

wrapped, return the shoulder to the smoker and cook for another 4 to 6 hours or until the internal temperature reaches 198° to 203°F. Don't be afraid to poke the thermometer through the wrapping, just do it on the top side so the juices don't run out.

Once the shoulder reaches the desired internal temperature, the meat should have reached the perfect degree of texture and doneness. A visual sign of the shoulder being appropriately cooked is that the bone can be easily removed just by pulling on it. Remove the shoulder from the smoker and set aside in a warm spot to rest for 1 hour.

Unwrap the pork shoulder and "punch" (a pitmaster's term for "shred") the meat to the desired size and texture. Garnish with a sprinkle of barbecue seasoning and serve with the barbecue sauce on the side.

While the turkey is marinating, using cherry wood, preheat your smoker to 250°F.

Place a thermometer probe in the center of the turkey breast and place the seasoned breast in the smoker, away from the heat source. Smoke for 1 hour or until the internal temperature reads 100°F.

Remove the turkey from the smoker, take out the probe, and wrap the entire breast in butcher paper. Place the probe back into the meat and return the meat to the smoker. Cook for an additional 1 hour to 90 minutes or until the internal temperature reaches 140°F (see BBQ Bits & Pieces). Remove the turkey from the smoker and transfer to an insulated space, such as a sealed cooler (see BBQ Bits & Pieces). Allow it to rest for 1 hour without opening the container.

When ready to serve, remove the breast from the insulated container, unwrap, and cut into even slices.

BBQ BITS & PIECES: Many of you may also be wondering why we don't cook turkey breast to 165°F as usually recommended. This is because bacteria are killed over a ratio of time to temperature. The most common way of eliminating the threat of salmonella and other pathogenic bacteria is to cook the poultry to an internal temperature of 165°F, at which point the bacteria instantly dies. However, bacteria are also destroyed if a certain temperature is sustained for a precise period of time. In the case of this recipe, the FDA says that the threat of bacterial contamination is eliminated when poultry is kept at 140°F for a minimum of 12 minutes. Thus, transferring the turkey to an insulated container for an hour will maintain 140°F for this prescribed longer time period. This allows the meat to retain its juiciness, kills the bacteria, and results in tender, flavorful meat.

CHIPOTLE-RUBBED BEER CAN CHICKEN

Beer can chicken is an all-time favorite, and when it is smoked, it is even better than that backyard sensation. Inevitably, the chickens fall over during cooking; it's okay . . . It happens to all of us. Although we love having a sip or two from the can before we use the beer, there are nifty gadgets that can be purchased online that aid in holding the chicken upright to give more stability when cooking. If this recipe becomes a regular on your menu, that gadget is worth the investment.

SERVES 4 TO 6

2 (3½-pound) chickens, giblets removed

1 gallon Standard Brine (page 69)

2 tablespoons Pre-Seasoning Rub (page 45)

4 tablespoons Chipotle Barbecue Rub (page 47)

2 (12-ounce) cans beer, your favorite brand

2 cups Honey-Chipotle Dipping Sauce (page 61)

Place the chickens in whatever container or resealable plastic bag you have chosen to brine them in. Add the brine, taking care that the chickens are completely covered. (It is extremely important that the birds be totally submerged; if you don't have one large container, brine the chickens separately.) Transfer to the refrigerator and brine for at least 4 hours or up to 8 hours.

Place a wire rack on a rimmed baking sheet. Remove the chickens from the refrigerator and discard the brine. Place the chickens on the wire rack and, using paper towels, pat them dry.

Using 1 tablespoon of the pre-seasoning rub for each chicken, lightly coat the exterior. Allow to rest at room temperature for 30 minutes, then season each chicken with 2 tablespoons of the chipotle rub and allow to rest at room temperature for 30 minutes more.

While the chickens are resting, using cherry wood (or your favorite wood), preheat your smoker to 250°F.

Open both cans of beer and, if you are in the mood, drink about a quarter of each one. Otherwise, pour it out, leaving the can with enough liquid to stabilize it.

ooo *continued*

Working with one at a time, carefully place a chicken on each beer can, taking care that it is quite stable. Insert a thermometer probe into a thigh of each chicken, hitting just where it meets the bone, then carefully transfer the entire package—beer can, chicken, and probes—into the smoker. Smoke for 2 hours or until the internal temperature of the thigh reaches 175°F.

Put on your gloves (see page 38) and remove the chickens from the smoker. Place them on a platter or tray, with each bird resting on its beer can. Let stand for 10 minutes.

Again using gloves, carefully remove the chickens from the cans and place them on a cutting board. Discard the cans (and any beer inside).

Using your butchering skills, cut the chicken into legs, thighs, wings, and breasts for serving. Place the pieces on a serving platter and serve with the honey-chipotle sauce.

BBQ BITS & PIECES: Extra-large resealable plastic bags are terrific to use for brining, as they allow for much easier refrigeration space management. However, if you don't have room in your refrigerator, you can use a cooler. Place ice cubes in the brine solution and store the chickens in the cooler for the required minimum 4 hours of brining. As long as the temperature of the water stays at or below 40°F, this is a perfectly safe method to use.

YANKEE RED HOT SAUSAGES WITH JEFF'S PEPPS
(FEATURING GRANDMA VAL'S SWEET ITALIAN SAUSAGE)

Matt grew up eating sausage heros garnished with provolone cheese and pickled cherry peppers. He always talked about how cool it would be to mix the condiments into the sausage. He first developed our recipe to enter into the "exotic" category at Memphis in May. He worked with our partner, Rob Shawger, creating many iterations of the final product. When they got a mix they loved, they began sharing it. Everyone who had a taste was blown away when they saw the cheese slowly oozing from the sausage as it came out of the smoker! Not only was it visually inviting, the flavors wowed with the perfect balance of juicy sausage and the bright, vinegary crunch of the peppers. Of course, the molten provolone cheese was the icing on the cake (so to speak).

At the 2016 Memphis in May, this dish placed in the top ten in the exotic category, and it is now a staple on the Pig Beach menu as the Yankee Red Hot.

The base of this recipe is Matt's grandma Val's sweet Italian sausage, which makes about 2 pounds. You can turn it into eight to ten links, as we do at Pig Beach, or use it in other ways as loose sausage meat or formed into patties. If you have a meat grinder or a grinder attachment for your stand mixer, this is your opportunity to give it a workout, should you want to grind your own pork; otherwise, just purchase ground pork.

SERVES 4 TO 6

Place the ground pork in a chilled large bowl. Add the wine, salt, sugar, parsley, garlic, fennel, onion, black pepper, and oregano and, using your hands, mix for about 10 minutes or until the mixture is completely blended and has the texture of raw sausage meat. This seems like a long time to mix, but it is necessary to create the texture you are looking for. When ready, the mixture should be very tacky and stick to the palm of your hand without crumbling or breaking up. Cover the

ooo continued

2 pounds 75% lean ground pork shoulder, ice-cold (see BBQ Bits & Pieces)

2 tablespoons dry white wine

2 tablespoons kosher salt

1 tablespoon sugar

2 teaspoons dried parsley

2 teaspoons granulated garlic

2 teaspoons ground fennel seed

1 teaspoon granulated onion

1 teaspoon café grind black pepper (see page 73)

½ teaspoon dried oregano

4 ounces provolone cheese, cut into small cubes

3 tablespoons medium-diced pickled cherry peppers (see BBQ Bits & Pieces)

1 pack pre-tubed 35–38mm natural hog casings (see BBQ Bits & Pieces)

1 cup Jeff's Pepps (page 98)

World Champion Mustard Sauce (page 51), for serving

bowl with plastic wrap and refrigerate for at least 1 hour or up to 4 hours before making links.

Add the provolone and cherry peppers to the meat mixture. Mix for about 5 minutes to incorporate the add-ins as well as to regain the tacky texture. Cover again and refrigerate for 1 hour.

While the sausage mix is chilling, prepare a sausage stuffer tube with the hog casings.

Transfer the chilled sausage meat into the hopper of the sausage stuffer. Bring the hog casing to the end of the stuffing tube and tie it into a knot. Begin cranking the sausage stuffer with your right hand while using your left hand to control the casing and the amount of meat being stuffed into it. The casing must be taut with the filling, but not so full that the casing bursts when it is twisted into links.

Continue to crank the sausage meat into the casing, rolling the meat-filled casing into a pinwheel as you go. When all the sausage meat has been stuffed into the casing, leaving enough slack to tie a knot, cut the casing from the stuffing tube. Tie a knot to secure the end of the sausage rope, then, using a sausage pricker or a metal cake tester, poke little holes all throughout the casing to allow any trapped air to escape.

Place a wire rack on a rimmed baking sheet. Using your hands, twist the sausage rope at roughly 5-inch intervals to create individual 4- to 6-ounce links. Transfer the links to the wire rack and refrigerate, uncovered, for 12 hours. This refrigeration is an important step as it makes the casing adhere to the sausage, as well as allows the magic of the mix to develop the perfect sausage texture. (At this point, the links can be transferred to the freezer until frozen, then packed into resealable freezer bags and stored in the freezer for up to 2 months for later use.)

When ready to cook, using cherry wood, preheat your smoker to 250°F.

Place the sausages in the smoker and cook for about 1 hour or until the internal temperature reaches 155°F. Remove the sausages from the smoker and place on a wire rack to rest for 10 minutes.

While the sausage is resting, clean and oil the grill grate and preheat the grill to high (see pages 130–131).

Place the sausages on the hot grill and grill for 1 minute. Flip and grill on the second side for another minute. You just want to develop the char marks, not really cook the sausage as it has already been cooked through in the smoker.

Transfer the sausage to a cutting board and cut into pieces, or place into your favorite hot dog roll (at Pig Beach, we use Martin's potato rolls) and top with Jeff's Pepps and mustard sauce, if you like.

BBQ BITS & PIECES: Pork shoulder usually has the magical ratio of 75% meat to 25% fat that is perfect for making sausage. We prefer grinding the shoulder ourselves so we can keep an eye on the desired ratio. If the ground meat is too lean, the finished sausage will be dry. If it's too fatty, the sausage will be greasy and might explode during cooking. That being said, you can, of course, buy 75% lean ground pork if you don't have a meat grinder.

When grinding meat for sausage, it is important to keep the meat very, very cold. We cut pork shoulder into 1-inch cubes and freeze the cubes for 1 hour before grinding. This prevents the fat from melting as the grinder heats up and when the meat is mixed with other ingredients with warm hands. The cubes should be ground using a ¼-inch plate directly into a chilled bowl.

At Pig Beach, we use B&G brand vinegar cherry peppers, but any fine-quality pickled cherry peppers will work.

Natural hog casings are available online or at any sausage-making store.

JEFF'S PEPPS

MAKES 2 CUPS

1 tablespoon vegetable oil

1 garlic clove, minced

2 cups finely diced red bell pepper

½ cup finely diced red onion

½ cup red wine vinegar

½ cup sugar

1½ tablespoons whole-grain mustard

¼ cup chopped cherry peppers (see page 97)

½ teaspoon kosher salt

Heat the vegetable oil in a small saucepan over medium heat. Add the garlic and cook, stirring frequently, for about 2 minutes or just until golden brown. Add the bell pepper and onion and cook, stirring frequently, for about 5 minutes or until the vegetables are a bit soft but still slightly crunchy.

Stir in the vinegar, sugar, and mustard until well blended, then add the cherry peppers and season with salt. Bring to a simmer and cook at a gentle simmer for about 10 minutes or until the liquid thickens and becomes syrupy. Remove from the heat and set aside to cool. When cool, transfer to a nonreactive container, cover, and store in the refrigerator for up to 1 month.

PORK RIBS CHAR SIU

The inspiration for these ribs came from our partner, the one and only Rob Shawger. After a meal at his favorite Chinese restaurant, Wu's Wonton King on Manhattan's Lower East Side, Rob asked if we thought it would be possible to get all the deep flavor and color of the restaurant's pork char siu on a baby back rib. We replied, why not? We immediately began R&D on the flavor profiles and techniques of this classic Chinese preparation. We believe that we developed something really special with this recipe; it truly has all that incredible flavor and color of the traditional Chinese dish, but with the added smoky hit of traditional barbecue.

SERVES 4 TO 6

Using cherry wood, preheat your smoker to 250°F.

Pat the ribs dry using paper towels, then season both sides of the racks with the rub. Set aside to rest for 15 minutes.

Place the ribs in the smoker at the point farthest away from the heat source. Smoke for 2 hours, basting with the char siu sauce every 20 minutes.

Remove the ribs from the smoker and place them on a large piece of heavy-duty aluminum foil. Add ¼ cup of the char siu sauce and tightly wrap the foil around them. Return the ribs to the smoker and smoke for 1 hour, then baste the ribs with the char siu sauce to create a lacquered red appearance. Cook for another 30 minutes or until the internal temperature at the thickest part of the meat reaches 198° to 200°F and the bones become easy to wiggle. Remove from the smoker and set aside in a warm spot to rest for 20 minutes.

Remove the foil and serve warm, with the barbecue sauce and chile oil.

2 (2½-pound) racks loin back pork ribs

2 tablespoons Pre-Seasoning Rub (page 45)

2 cups Char Siu Sauce (page 108)

1 cup Nee Family Chinese Barbecue Sauce (page 109)

¼ cup Sichuan Chile Oil (page 110)

CHAR SIU SAUCE

MAKES 2 CUPS

½ cup tamari

½ cup honey

½ cup ketchup

⅓ cup light brown sugar

2 garlic cloves, microplaned (see BBQ Bits & Pieces on page 110)

2 tablespoons rice vinegar

2 tablespoons hoisin sauce

1 tablespoon oyster sauce

1 teaspoon five-spice powder

1 tablespoon red food coloring (optional)

Combine the tamari, honey, ketchup, and sugar in a medium saucepan. Stir in the garlic, vinegar, hoisin, oyster sauce, and five-spice powder. Bring to a simmer over medium heat, then reduce the heat to low and cook, stirring frequently, for about 5 minutes or until the sauce has thickened. Stir in the food coloring (if using). Cook for another minute or so to blend well. Remove from the heat and transfer to a nonreactive container. Set aside to cool.

Use immediately or cover and store in the refrigerator for up to 1 month.

NEE FAMILY CHINESE BARBECUE SAUCE

MAKES ABOUT 4 CUPS

Heat the oil in a large heavy-bottomed saucepan over medium-low heat. Add the scallions, star anise, and five-spice powder and cook, stirring frequently, for about 7 minutes or until the scallions are very soft. Add the garlic and ginger and cook for about 7 minutes or until very aromatic and tender. Do not allow to brown; if the garlic and ginger are beginning to color, reduce the heat.

Add the hoisin, reduce the heat to low, and cook, stirring occasionally, for about 30 minutes or until well blended and thick. Remove from the heat and pour through a fine-mesh sieve into a clean container. Discard the solids. Stir in the vinegar and tamari and set aside to cool.

Use immediately or transfer to a nonreactive container, cover, and store in the refrigerator for up to 1 month.

¼ cup vegetable oil

1 bunch scallions, white parts only, thinly sliced

8 star anise pods

2 tablespoons five-spice powder

¼ cup finely minced garlic (about 1 head)

¼ cup minced fresh ginger

4 cups hoisin sauce

¼ cup black vinegar

2 tablespoons tamari

BBQ BITS & PIECES: Kim Nee was the opening pitmaster at Pig Beach. He had a long culinary pedigree, having worked in some of the country's best restaurants and resorts as well as for celebrity chefs, including Bobby Flay. From the very first days of cooking under a pop-up tent in a parking lot (through monsoons and thunderstorms), Kim has stayed with us. There is nothing better than getting inspiration from your team, and Kim is always there for us. This sauce is one of his family secrets, but he was happy to share it with us for this book, so we named it in his honor.

SICHUAN CHILE OIL

MAKES 2 CUPS

2 cups
vegetable oil

2 garlic cloves,
peeled

1 shallot

3 star anise
pods

1 cinnamon
stick

1 bay leaf

2 teaspoons
kosher salt

¾ cup ground
Sichuan chile
flakes (see
BBQ Bits &
Pieces)

Heat the oil in a medium saucepan over medium heat. Add the garlic, shallot, star anise, cinnamon stick, and bay leaf. Cook for about 12 minutes or until the oil mixture reaches 225°F on an instant read thermometer. Keeping the temperature at 225°F cook for an additional 10 minutes. This allows the aromatics and spices to infuse the oil.

When the oil is heating, place the Sichuan chile flakes in a heat proof, nonreactive container.

When the oil is ready, place a fine-mesh strainer over the chile flakes. Pour the hot oil through the strainer over the chile flakes. The oil will froth slightly when it hits the chile flakes, which is desirable. Discard the solids.

Set the oil aside to cool. When cool, pour into a nonreactive container, cover, and store in the refrigerator for up to 6 months.

BBQ BITS & PIECES: A Microplane grater, also called a rasp grater, is an indispensable kitchen tool. In this recipe, it turns the garlic into a paste with just a few runs across the grater's teeth, which allows the garlic to be easily incorporated into the mixture.

If you don't want to add the extra step of making the chile oil, you can replace it with a fine-quality Asian chile oil, available from Asian markets, specialty food stores, some supermarkets, and online.

Sichuan chile flakes are available from some Asian markets or online.

MOJO MARINADE

MAKES 3 CUPS

Place the garlic, cilantro, and onion in a blender. Add the olive oil, orange, lemon juice, lime juice, oregano, salt, and cumin. Blend on high for about 3 minutes or until smooth.

Transfer to a nonreactive container, cover, and store in the refrigerator for up to 3 days.

9 garlic cloves, peeled

1 cup tightly packed fresh cilantro leaves

1 cup diced Spanish onion

¾ cup olive oil

½ cup fresh orange juice

¼ cup fresh lemon juice

¼ cup fresh lime juice

1 tablespoon dried oregano

2 teaspoons kosher salt

¾ teaspoon ground cumin

MOJO VERDE SAUCE

MAKES ABOUT 2 CUPS

Place the garlic and cilantro in a blender. Add the vinegar, egg yolk, jalapeño, salt, and cumin and blend on medium just until smooth. Increase the blender speed to high and, with the motor running, begin adding the oil. Blend until the mixture becomes a smooth, creamy, green emulsion. Add the water, a bit at a time, if necessary to thin the sauce.

Transfer to a nonreactive container, cover, and store in the refrigerator for up to 1 week.

2 garlic cloves, peeled

½ cup tightly packed fresh cilantro leaves

½ cup white vinegar

1 tablespoon pasteurized egg yolk

2 teaspoons minced jalapeño

1 teaspoon kosher salt

⅛ teaspoon ground cumin

¾ cup vegetable oil

1 tablespoon water

MOJO ROJO SAUCE

MAKES 2 CUPS

2 guajillo chiles, stemmed and seeded (see BBQ Bits & Pieces)

1 pasilla chile, stemmed and seeded (see BBQ Bits & Pieces)

12 garlic cloves, peeled

½ cup white vinegar

1 tablespoon honey

1 tablespoon smoked paprika

2 teaspoons kosher salt

1 teaspoon ground cumin

1 cup vegetable oil

Heat a medium skillet over medium heat. When hot, add the guajillo and pasilla chiles and cook, turning frequently, for about 2 minutes or until they are nicely toasted, very fragrant, and have released their natural oils.

Place the garlic in a small saucepan. Add the toasted chiles and 1 cup water. Bring to a simmer over medium-high heat. Immediately reduce the heat to maintain a gentle simmer and cook for 5 minutes. Remove from the heat and drain through a fine-mesh sieve, reserving the cooking liquid.

Place the garlic and chiles in a blender. Add the vinegar, honey, paprika, salt, and cumin along with ½ cup of the reserved cooking liquid. Blend to a smooth puree.

With the motor running, begin adding the oil in a slow, steady stream. Continue adding the oil until the mixture is slightly thickened and well emulsified. If the mixture is too thick, add some of the reserved cooking liquid a teaspoon at a time until the desired consistency is reached. Transfer to a nonreactive container and set aside to cool.

When cool, cover and store in the refrigerator for up to 1 month.

BBQ BITS & PIECES: Guajillo and pasilla chiles are available from Mexican markets, specialty food stores, some supermarkets, and online.

CARIBBEAN JERK RIBS WITH MANGO-SCOTCH BONNET BARBECUE SAUCE

Brooklyn, New York, home to the first Pig Beach, is also home to many, many people of Caribbean descent. So much so, that it has a major West Indian festival once a year, during which jerk chicken or pork will always be on the barbecue. Although jerk seasoning is usually linked to Jamaica, some version of this pungent sweet-hot mix can be found on other islands throughout the Caribbean, as well as on the streets and in the cafés of Brooklyn.

SERVES 4 TO 6

Using cherry wood, preheat your smoker to 250°F.

Pat the ribs dry using paper towels, then season both sides of the racks with the rub, using 1 tablespoon for each rack. Set aside to rest for 15 minutes, then evenly season both sides of the racks with the Caribbean jerk rub.

Place the ribs in the smoker at the point farthest away from the heat source. Smoke for 2 hours, spritzing with the barbecue spritz every 20 minutes.

Remove the ribs from the smoker and place them on a large piece of heavy-duty aluminum foil. Tightly wrap the foil around them. Return the ribs to the smoker and smoke for 1 hour to 90 minutes or until the internal temperature at the thickest part of the meat reaches 198° to 200°F and the bones become easy to wiggle. Remove from the smoker and set aside in a warm spot to rest for 20 minutes.

Remove the foil and serve warm, drizzled with the barbecue sauce.

2 (2½-pound) racks loin back pork ribs

2 tablespoons Pre-Seasoning Rub (page 45)

1 cup Caribbean Jerk Rub (page 121)

3 cups All-Purpose Barbecue Spritz (page 68)

2 cups Mango–Scotch Bonnet Barbecue Sauce (page 122)

CARIBBEAN JERK RUB

MAKES 1 CUP

Combine the onion, garlic, sugar, and parsley in a small bowl. Add the salt, paprika, cayenne, thyme, allspice, black pepper, cumin, nutmeg, cinnamon, chile flakes, and cloves and stir vigorously to blend.

Transfer to an airtight container, cover, and store at room temperature for up to 3 months.

2 tablespoons granulated onion

2 tablespoons granulated garlic

2 tablespoons light brown sugar

2 tablespoons dried parsley

1 tablespoon kosher salt

1 tablespoon paprika

2 teaspoons cayenne pepper

2 teaspoons dried thyme

2 teaspoons ground allspice

2 teaspoons ground black pepper

1 teaspoon ground cumin

1 teaspoon ground nutmeg

1 teaspoon ground cinnamon

1 teaspoon chile flakes

½ teaspoon ground cloves

MANGO-SCOTCH BONNET BARBECUE SAUCE

MAKES 1 QUART

1 Scotch bonnet pepper (see BBQ Bits & Pieces)

2 cups mango puree

1 cup ketchup

¼ cup apple cider vinegar

¼ cup honey

¼ cup light brown sugar

2 tablespoons key lime juice

2 tablespoons yellow mustard

2 tablespoons molasses

1 tablespoon granulated onion

1 tablespoon Worcestershire sauce

2 teaspoons ground ginger

2 teaspoons kosher salt

½ teaspoon granulated garlic

Wearing nitrile gloves, stem and seed the Scotch bonnet. Using a sharp knife, finely dice the pepper. Set aside.

Combine the mango puree, ketchup, vinegar, honey, and sugar in a medium saucepan. Stir in the lime juice, mustard, molasses, onion, Worcestershire, ginger, salt, and garlic. Bring to a simmer over medium heat, stirring occasionally.

Add the Scotch bonnet, reduce the heat to maintain a bare simmer, and cook for 5 minutes. Remove the sauce from the heat and, using an immersion blender, blend to a smooth puree.

Set aside to cool.

Transfer to a nonreactive container, cover, and store in the refrigerator for up to 1 month.

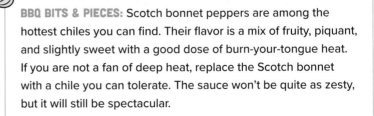

BBQ BITS & PIECES: Scotch bonnet peppers are among the hottest chiles you can find. Their flavor is a mix of fruity, piquant, and slightly sweet with a good dose of burn-your-tongue heat. If you are not a fan of deep heat, replace the Scotch bonnet with a chile you can tolerate. The sauce won't be quite as zesty, but it will still be spectacular.

HOT HONEY ST. LOUIS RIBS

This recipe is another one that caught the attention of our friends at Hormel Foods. After the huge success of the cobranded Pig Beach & Lloyd's Pulled Pork as well as the pulled chicken ready-to-eat barbecue line, Hormel asked us to create a new and exciting rub for their fresh pork division to feature. This Hot Honey Rub blew the team away with its perfect balance of sweet and heat. It will soon be available on a Hormel pork sparerib in grocery stores across the country.

The rub is also amazing tossed with peanuts. Lightly coat peanuts with the rub, then place the seasoned peanuts in a single layer on a parchment-lined rimmed baking sheet. Bake at 250°F for about 15 minutes or until the peanuts are nicely glazed and crisp.

SERVES 4 TO 6

Using cherry wood, preheat your smoker to 250°F.

Pat the ribs dry using paper towels, then sprinkle both sides of the racks with the seasoning. Set aside to rest for 15 minutes.

Generously coat both sides of the racks with some of the hot honey rub. Set aside to marinate at room temperature for 20 minutes.

Place the ribs in the smoker at the point farthest away from the heat source. Smoke for 2 hours, spritzing with the barbecue spritz every 20 minutes.

Remove the ribs from the smoker and place them on a large piece of heavy-duty aluminum foil. Top each rack with 1 tablespoon of the drizzle and 1 tablespoon of the butter. Tightly wrap the foil around them. Return the ribs to the smoker and smoke for 1 hour to 90 minutes or until the internal temperature at the thickest part of the meat reaches 198° to 200°F and the bones become easy to wiggle. Remove from the smoker and set aside in a warm spot to rest for 20 minutes.

Remove the foil and serve warm with the remaining Hot Honey Drizzle.

2 racks St. Louis–cut pork spareribs

¼ cup All-Purpose Barbecue Seasoning (page 44)

3 cups Pig Beach Hot Honey Rub (page 124)

½ cup Hot Honey Drizzle (page 124)

All-Purpose Barbecue Spritz (page 68)

2 tablespoons unsalted butter

PIG BEACH HOT HONEY RUB

MAKES 3 CUPS

2 cups All-Purpose Barbecue Seasoning (page 44)

1 cup granulated honey

¼ teaspoon ghost pepper chile powder (see BBQ Bits & Pieces)

Taking care to be in a well-ventilated area, because the fumes from the chile powder are quite noxious, combine the seasoning, honey, and chile powder in a small bowl and stir until thoroughly blended.

Transfer to a nonreactive container, cover, and store in a cool, dark spot for up to 1 month.

HOT HONEY DRIZZLE

MAKES ABOUT ½ CUP

½ cup honey

2 teaspoons Pig Beach Hot Honey Rub (above)

⅛ teaspoon ghost pepper chile powder (see BBQ Bits & Pieces)

Taking care to be in a well-ventilated area because the fumes from the chile powder are quite noxious, combine the honey, rub, and chile powder in a small bowl and stir until thoroughly blended.

Transfer to a nonreactive container, cover, and store in a cool, dark spot for up to 1 month.

BBQ BITS & PIECES: Ghost pepper chile powder is available online. Be VERY CAREFUL when handling it. It can burn your nose, eyes, mouth, and hands, as well as any skin you might touch with your hands after touching the chile powder. Wear gloves while using it; remove and discard the gloves when you're finished, then wash your hands carefully.

Although it's great on ribs, the hot honey drizzle also does some amazing tricks on a pepperoni pizza!

CHINESE STICKY RIBS

You cannot live in NYC without having a love for Chinese food and culture. It is one of the most delicious and accessible cuisines for takeout and delivery, as well as one of the most affordable. Every New Yorker has their favorite Chinese restaurant, and it is often the first go-to when you're back in town from a vacation or business trip.

This recipe gets its inspiration from a couple of our favorite takeout meals, sesame chicken and General Tso's chicken. It embraces that crispy, sweet glaze we all know so well. Not only are these ribs crave-worthy, they are a great way to use up day-old cooked ribs. Serve them as an appetizer or a main.

SERVES 4 TO 6

4 cups vegetable oil

1 cup Fried Chicken Dredge (page 48)

1 rack cooked Loin Back Ribs with Peach and Honey Glaze (page 81), chilled

1½ cups Sticky Rib Glaze (opposite)

1 cup chopped unsalted peanuts or toasted sesame seeds, for garnish

¼ cup fresh cilantro leaves, for garnish

½ cup Pickled Red Onions (page 210), for garnish (optional)

Place the oil in a large heavy-bottomed saucepan over medium-high heat and bring to 350°F on an instant-read thermometer.

While the oil is heating, place the dredge in a large bowl. Remove the rib rack from the refrigerator. Using a sharp knife, cut the rack into individual ribs.

Transfer the ribs to the dredge and toss to coat well. Remove the coated ribs from the dredge and set aside on a platter.

Place the glaze in a large shallow bowl. Set aside.

Begin adding the ribs to the hot oil one at a time, taking care not to overload the pan or splash the oil. (We suggest frying no more than 6 ribs at a time to ensure they brown evenly.) Fry for about 4 minutes or until the coating is golden brown and the ribs are warmed through. Using a spider or a pair of tongs, carefully transfer the ribs to the bowl of glaze and toss to completely coat.

Serve immediately, garnished with peanuts or sesame seeds and cilantro. You might also want to add the pickled red onions for a pop of acid and color.

To continue with wood grilling, either make a small pile of kindling or break up a couple of fire-starter cubes in the center of the grill pan. Then build a tepee-shaped mound of very dry pieces of hardwood, such as hickory or oak, around the kindling. Use enough wood to create a nice thick layer of embers to generate the heat needed to grill successfully. Using a long fireplace match or an automatic lighter, ignite the kindling or fire-starter pieces.

Watch for a few minutes until the wood catches fire, then sit back and relax for half an hour or so while the wood burns and begins to turn into embers. It is important that you allow the wood to burn down, as you do not want to cook over raging flames. You want the calm, even heat that the embers provide. Using tongs or a small shovel, spread the embers out to an even layer.

For all methods of grilling, once the heat source has reached its optimum heat level, return the oiled grate to the grill and allow it to get hot. Then place the meat, fish, or vegetables (or whatever you are grilling) on the hot grate.

If you feel that wood grilling is more than you want to tackle for a Saturday backyard grill, you can use either lump charcoal or charcoal briquettes. Lump charcoal is wood that has been burned in the absence of oxygen, which removes the sap, moisture, and chemicals within the wood. The end result is a pure wood product that burns fast, clean, and hot. Briquettes are made from sawdust and bits of leftover woods that are also burned without oxygen but with additives to bind the mixture into the even cubes. Although these burn fast, they do not burn as hot as lump charcoal and they can sometimes flavor the grilled product with whatever additive has been used. Briquettes are generally less expensive than lump charcoal.

Propane gas grills are the cleanest and easiest to use, but they do not impart any smoky flavor whatsoever. They heat up very quickly and offer immediate temperature control; however, they are not much different from cooking on an indoor gas stove. We know that propane is what most backyard grills use these days, but this does not mean you can't adapt them to your personal choice.

We suggest that no matter the method used to grill, you set up what we call "zone" heating. This simply means that one section of the grill has high heat to create excellent char and flavor and another section radiates lower heat to finish the cooking without overcharring the exterior.

TEMPERATURE CHART FOR GRILLED MEATS

BEEF AND LAMB:

RARE: 125° TO 130°F

MEDIUM-RARE: 130° TO 135°F

MEDIUM: 135° TO 140°F

MEDIUM-WELL: 145° TO 150°F

WELL-DONE: 160°F

VEAL: 145° TO 155°F

POULTRY:

WHITE MEAT: 155° TO 160°F

DARK MEAT: 160° TO 165°F

If you don't have a thermometer and are unsure about the degree of doneness of your meat, you can place a metal cake tester into the thickest section for 5 seconds. Remove it and press it against your wrist or lip. If it feels cool, the meat is raw. If it is as warm as your skin, the meat is medium-rare. If it's very hot, the meat is well-done and probably now overcooked. Never cut into a piece of meat to test the doneness, as this will allow juices to escape as well as mar the look of the finished product. As a matter of fact, this is a great time to talk about the proper resting of meat, which can be the difference between a moist, succulent bite and a tough, dry one. ALWAYS, ALWAYS, ALWAYS REST THAT MEAT!!! From the thinnest steak to the biggest brisket, allowing the meat to rest and distribute its carryover heat and juices will give you the best bite. You should allow about 5 minutes for a thin steak or pork chop and 30 minutes to an hour for a large cut like a pork shoulder or brisket.

BACON–ONION MAGIC

MAKES ½ CUP

1 teaspoon vegetable oil

5 ounces sliced bacon, diced

1 teaspoon unsalted butter

1 medium Vidalia onion, sliced

3 tablespoons light brown sugar

2 tablespoons balsamic vinegar

¼ teaspoon chopped fresh thyme

¼ teaspoon salt

¼ teaspoon ground black pepper

Heat a large skillet over medium heat. When warm, add the oil. When the oil is hot, add the bacon and fry, stirring frequently, for about 10 minutes or until crisp. Using a slotted spatula, scoop the bacon from the pan and place on a double layer of paper towels to drain. Reserve 2 tablespoons of the rendered bacon fat in the pan. (Store any remaining fat for another use; it will keep, covered, in the refrigerator for months.)

Return the pan to medium heat and add the butter. When the butter has melted, add the onion. Reduce the heat to medium-low and cook, stirring occasionally, for about 15 minutes or until the onion is very soft and well caramelized.

Return the bacon to the pan and add the sugar, vinegar, and thyme. Season with salt and pepper and cook for about 10 minutes or until the mixture has a jamlike consistency. Remove from the heat.

Use immediately, or let cool, then transfer to a container, cover, and set aside until ready to use or store in the refrigerator for up to 1 week. Use at room temperature or warm slightly before using.

WHERE'S THE MEAT BURGER
(SMOKED PECAN, QUINOA, AND CHICKPEA PATTIES)

As much as we are meat-centric, we do have to accommodate our customers who choose not to eat animal protein. After much trial and error, we came up with this mix, which has great flavor and takes to the regular Pig Beach fixin's just like our meat-based burgers do.

If you choose not to smoke the pecans, you can either toast them on the stovetop in a heavy-bottomed pan over very low heat or roast, stirring occasionally, in a 300°F oven for about 6 minutes. However, we think that the smoke flavor elevates these meatless burgers in a most delicious way.

Serve these as is or just as we do our regular Pig Beach Burger (page 141), with sauce and pickles or with a slice of cheese melted over the top while the patties grill. Another tasty mix is sliced tomatoes, butter lettuce, and our NYC White Sauce (page 58).

MAKES 5

Using cherry wood, preheat your smoker to 250°F.

Line a small rimmed baking sheet with parchment paper. Spread the pecans in an even layer over the baking sheet and place the pan in the smoker. Smoke for 30 minutes or until nicely toasted and smoky. Remove from the smoker and set aside to cool.

When cool, using a sharp knife, chop the pecans into small pieces and set aside.

Place 2 quarts water and 1 tablespoon of the salt in a large saucepan. Bring to a boil over high heat. Add the quinoa and cook, stirring occasionally, for about 10 minutes or just until the quinoa is tender. Remove from the heat. Pour the quinoa into a strainer and set aside to drain well and cool slightly. You need to remove as much water as possible.

Spread the cooked quinoa in an even layer on a rimmed baking sheet and set aside to cool completely, then cover and refrigerate until ready to use.

½ cup pecan pieces

1 tablespoon plus ½ teaspoon kosher salt

⅓ cup uncooked quinoa

1 tablespoon vegetable oil

2 garlic cloves, minced

1 large red onion, finely diced

1 tablespoon tomato paste

2 teaspoons Dijon mustard

1½ teaspoons Worcestershire sauce

¾ teaspoon finely minced fresh thyme

1 cup finely chopped cooked or canned chickpeas

1½ teaspoons Pig Beach All-Purpose Barbecue Seasoning (page 44)

¼ teaspoon ground black pepper

ooo continued

Heat the oil in a small heavy-bottomed saucepan over medium heat. When warm, add the garlic and cook, stirring, for about 2 minutes or until light golden brown and very aromatic. Add the onion and cook, stirring occasionally, for about 20 minutes or until well caramelized. Add the tomato paste, mustard, Worcestershire, and thyme and cook, stirring occasionally, for another 5 minutes.

Line a small rimmed baking sheet with parchment paper. Scrape the onion mixture onto the prepared baking sheet and set aside to cool, then transfer to a large bowl.

Remove the quinoa from the refrigerator and add it to the onion mixture along with the pecans. Add the chickpeas and rib rub and season with the remaining ½ teaspoon salt and the pepper. Using your hands, blend the mixture well. Cover and refrigerate for at least 1 hour to allow the flavors to blend and to ensure the mixture will hold together when formed into patties.

Using your hands, form the chilled chickpea mixture into five 4-ounce patties. (At this point, if not cooking the patties immediately, you can place them on a parchment-lined plate or pan, cover, and refrigerate until ready to use, or place in the freezer until frozen, then transfer to a resealable freezer bag and freeze for up to 3 months. Defrost frozen patties before cooking.)

Clean and oil the grill grate and preheat the grill to high (see pages 130–131).

Grill the chickpea patties for 3 minutes, then flip and grill on the second side for 2 minutes. Serve immediately.

HATCH VINEGAR BARBECUE BUFFALO WINGS

Our diners think these are the best wings in the USA! Smoky, charred, sauced, and still room to dip in another sauce . . . add the carrot and celery sticks, and you have the best football-watching snack in the world.

If you choose to eliminate the smoking process, season as directed and proceed to grill as you would on whatever type grill you are using.

SERVES 4 TO 6

Rinse the wings and pat dry. Place in a large container, add the rub, and toss to coat. Set aside to dry brine for 30 minutes.

Add the poultry seasoning, toss to coat, and set aside for 15 minutes.

While the wings are resting, using cherry wood (or your favorite wood), preheat your smoker to 250°F.

Transfer the wings to the smoker, spacing them about ½ inch apart, and smoke for 1 hour or until the internal temperate reaches 165°F. Remove the wings from the smoker and place on a wire rack. Allow to rest for 10 minutes.

While the wings are resting, clean and oil the grill grate and preheat the grill, setting up high- and low-heat zones (see pages 130–131).

When the grill is very hot, place the wings in the high-heat zone and grill, turning once, for about 4 minutes or until they have a nice char on all sides. Move the wings to the low-heat zone, close the lid of the grill, and cook for an additional 5 minutes.

Place the barbecue sauce in a large bowl, then add the grilled wings and toss to coat in the sauce.

Place the wings on a platter or other serving plate and serve with Alabama white sauce or your favorite creamy, cheesy salad dressing, with carrot and celery sticks alongside, if desired.

3 pounds jumbo party chicken wings (about 3 dozen)

1 tablespoon Pre-Seasoning Rub (page 45)

½ cup Pig Beach Poultry Seasoning (page 45)

3 cups Barbecue Buffalo Wing Sauce (page 55)

2 cups Alabama White Sauce (page 59), for serving

2 cups carrot sticks, for serving (optional)

2 cups celery sticks, for serving (optional)

GRILLED OYSTERS WITH SPICY GARLIC BUTTER AND PARMESAN BREAD CRUMBS

These oysters are quite spicy, but oh, so delicious! You can use any type of oyster that appeals to you although you might want to get fairly large, meaty ones to hold in the oyster juices in the larger shell. At Pig Beach, we prefer a medium to large East Coast oyster, such as Island Creek oysters from Duxbury, Massachusetts. They have just the right amount of brininess to work with all the spicy goodness. Memphis in May wouldn't be the same without our yearly oyster night! The oysters also make an inviting appetizer at a backyard get-together.

MAKES 12

Clean and oil the grill grate and preheat the grill to high (see pages 130–131).

Place the oysters on a large rimmed baking sheet, then place an even amount of garlic butter on top of each oyster. Sprinkle with an even amount of bread crumbs. While seasoning the oysters, take care not to spill out any of their liquid.

Transfer the oysters, one at a time, to the hot grill; again, take care not to spill their liquid. Close the lid and grill for about 4 minutes or until the butter has melted into the oyster liquid and the bread crumbs have begun to brown lightly.

Using tongs, carefully remove the oysters from the grill and transfer to a serving platter. Sprinkle with the parsley. Serve immediately, with lemon wedges on the side.

12 fresh oysters, shucked and on the half shell, reserving as much liquid as possible

Spicy Garlic Butter (page 154)

Oreganato Bread Crumbs (page 154)

1 tablespoon chopped fresh flat-leaf parsley

Lemon wedges, for serving

SPICY GARLIC BUTTER

MAKES 1 CUP

1 cup (2 sticks) unsalted butter, at room temperature

Zest and juice of 1 lemon

3 garlic cloves, microplaned (see page 110)

2 anchovy fillets, minced

2 tablespoons sambal oelek (see page 127)

2 tablespoons sriracha (see page 127)

1 teaspoon fine sea salt

¼ teaspoon cayenne pepper

Place the butter in a medium bowl. Add the lemon zest, lemon juice, anchovies, sambal oelek, sriracha, salt, and cayenne. Using a wooden spoon, beat vigorously to blend completely.

Use immediately or transfer to a food-safe container, cover, and store in the refrigerator until ready to use, or up to 1 week. Bring to room temperature before using.

OREGANATO BREAD CRUMBS

MAKES ½ CUP

¼ cup grated Parmesan cheese

¼ cup panko bread crumbs

¾ teaspoon dried oregano

½ teaspoon garlic powder

½ cup chopped flat-leaf parsley

¼ teaspoon lemon zest

Pinch of chile flakes

Combine the cheese and bread crumbs in a small mixing bowl. Add the oregano, garlic powder, parsley, lemon zest, and chile flakes, stirring to blend well.

Use immediately or place in a food-safe container, cover, and store in the refrigerator for up to 2 days.

ELOTES (MEXICAN STREET CORN)

Elote, **which simply means "corncob" in Spanish, is the name this street corn is sold by in Mexico. It is usually sold with the husks pulled back to form a handle so the corn can be quickly eaten on the street. The rich and zesty coating turns summer corn into an amazing taste thrill.**

SERVES 6

Clean and oil the grill grate and preheat the grill to high (see pages 130–131).

Combine the sour cream, mayonnaise, cilantro, garlic, and lime zest and juice in a small bowl, whisking to combine thoroughly. Set aside.

Place the corn on the grill and grill for 2 minutes per side or until the entire ear is nicely charred. Remove the corn from the grill and transfer to a serving platter.

Using a pastry brush, generously coat each ear with the sour cream mixture. Crumble the cheese over the seasoned corn and then sprinkle with the seasoning.

Serve with the lime wedges on the side.

½ cup sour cream

½ cup mayonnaise

½ cup chopped fresh cilantro

1 garlic clove, minced

Zest and juice of 1 lime

6 ears corn, husks removed

1 cup crumbled Cotija cheese (see BBQ Bits & Pieces)

1 tablespoon All-Purpose Barbecue Seasoning (page 44)

6 lime wedges

BBQ BITS & PIECES: Cotija cheese is a salty cow's-milk cheese originating from the town of Cotija in Mexico. It is available from some supermarkets, specialty food stores, and Mexican markets, and online.

BEYOND BARBECUE

Smoked Duck Lasagna

Brisket Ravioli with Truffle Butter and Red Wine Jelly

The Beef Rib Gnocchi Matt Taught Chris Lilly

Smoked and Grilled Heritage Pork Chop with Peach-Habanero Jam

Shane's "Pastramen"

Smoked Chicken Thigh Potpie

Smoked Tomato Water–Poached Cod with Gingered Bok Choy

ravioli can be placed in the freezer until frozen, then transferred to a resealable plastic bag and stored in the freezer for up the 3 months. Cook directly from frozen (do not thaw, or the dough will become sticky and the ravioli will disintegrate). They should take about 10 minutes to cook.

FRESH EGG YOLK PASTA

MAKES 2 POUNDS

Place the 00, durum, and semolina flours in the bowl of a stand mixer fitted with the paddle attachment. Add the egg yolks and egg and mix on low for about 5 minutes or until the mixture begins to form a ball. Continue beating on low for an additional 10 minutes, adding water a tiny bit at a time, if needed, to fully work out the gluten in the flours. Remove the bowl from the mixer, cover with plastic wrap, and set aside at room temperature to rest for at least 30 minutes to relax the gluten strands in the dough.

Affix the pasta roller attachment to the stand mixer. Lightly flour a clean work surface. Cut the dough in half; enclose one half in plastic wrap and set aside. Place the remaining half on the floured surface. Using a rolling pin, roll the dough into a layer thin enough to fit in the pasta roller.

Begin running the dough through the pasta roller, beginning with the widest setting and progressively moving the dial until you've reached one notch before the thinnest setting, dusting the sheet with 00 flour as you go. As each sheet of pasta dough is finished, dust the sheet with flour and cover with plastic wrap until ready to use. Repeat to roll out the remaining dough.

3½ cups plus 2 tablespoons 00 flour, plus more for dusting (see page 175)

1½ cups durum flour

⅓ cup semolina flour

3 large egg yolks, at room temperature

1 large egg, at room temperature

Water, as needed

RED WINE JELLY

MAKES 1 CUP

2 cups dry red wine

2 tablespoons sugar

2 teaspoons apple pectin (see page 60)

½ teaspoon kosher salt

¼ teaspoon ground black pepper

2 teaspoons sherry vinegar

Place the wine in a nonreactive medium saucepan and bring to a boil over medium-high heat. Boil for about 20 minutes or until reduced to 1 cup.

Combine the sugar with the pectin in a small bowl and stir to blend completely.

When the wine has reduced, reduce the heat to medium and whisk in the sugar mixture, salt, and pepper. Return the mixture to a boil. When tightly formed bubbles start to rise to the surface, remove from the heat and whisk in the vinegar. Set aside to cool to room temperature.

Use immediately or transfer to a food-safe container, cover, and store in the refrigerator for up to 1 month. Reheat before serving.

THE BEEF RIB GNOCCHI MATT TAUGHT CHRIS LILLY

Chris Lilly, pitmaster supreme, knows much more about barbecue than we do. But he doesn't know a lot about Italian food, so Matt thought he'd teach him a thing or two by incorporating barbecue into a traditional Italian dish. The result? This deliciously rich and satisfying gnocchi with a hint of smoke in a classic Italian sauce.

SERVES 6 TO 8

Bring a large saucepan of salted water to a boil over high heat.

Meanwhile, heat the oil in a large sauté pan over medium heat. When it begins to ripple, stir in the garlic. Cook, stirring occasionally, for about 2 minutes or until golden brown. Add the shallots and cook for about 5 minutes or until the shallots are very soft and lightly caramelized. Do not burn.

Add the wine and cook for another 7 minutes or until reduced by half. Add the stock and stir to blend, then add the beef and bring to a simmer. Simmer for about 5 minutes to allow the flavors to blend and to warm the beef.

Reduce the heat to medium-low and stir in the butter. Cook, stirring, for another minute or so or until the butter has emulsified. Immediately reduce the heat as low as it can go and keep the sauce warm until ready to use.

Using a bench scraper or a flat spatula, transfer the gnocchi to the boiling water. Cook for about 2 minutes or until they begin to float. Using a slotted spoon, lift the gnocchi from the water and immediately place in the hot sauce.

When all the gnocchi have been added, raise the heat and gently cook for a minute or two to coat the gnocchi. Add ¼ cup of the cheese and 1 tablespoon of the parsley, gently stirring to blend.

Remove from the heat and divide among six pasta bowls. Garnish with the remaining cheese and parsley. Serve immediately.

2 tablespoons olive oil

8 garlic cloves, sliced

1 cup finely diced shallots

1 cup dry red wine

3 cups beef stock or low-sodium beef broth

1 pound leftover smoked beef rib meat (see page 83), chopped

½ cup (1 stick) unsalted butter

2 pounds Potato Gnocchi (page 174; or use store-bought)

½ cup grated Parmesan cheese

2 tablespoons chopped fresh flat-leaf parsley

POTATO GNOCCHI

MAKES 3 POUNDS

6 medium
Idaho potatoes

2 tablespoons
kosher salt

3 large eggs,
at room
temperature

1 egg yolk,
at room
temperature

2½ cups all-
purpose flour,
plus more for
dusting

Place the potatoes in a large saucepan and add cold water to cover by at least 1 inch. Add the salt and bring to a simmer over high heat. Simmer for about 20 minutes or until the potatoes are very tender. Remove from the heat and drain in a fine-mesh strainer. Set aside until cool enough to handle.

Lightly flour a clean work surface. When the potatoes are still hot but cool enough to handle, peel them and, working as quickly as you can, begin pushing them through a ricer (see BBQ Bits & Pieces) onto the prepared work surface, keeping them in an even layer.

When all the potatoes have been riced, let them rest for about 30 minutes or until very cool and dry. You need them to be as dry as possible so you can add as little flour as possible to keep the gnocchi from turning gummy or tough when cooked.

Combine the eggs with the egg yolk in a small bowl, whisking to blend completely. Pour the eggs over the potatoes. Sprinkle 2 cups of the flour over the eggs and potatoes. Gently fold the mixture together until flour is well incorporated. Do not overmix! The dough should be slightly sticky but workable.

Form the dough into ball. At this point, it is a good idea to pull off a few ¾-inch pieces of dough, roll them into small balls and add them to boiling water. If the dough falls apart, begin to work in additional flour, then test again. Continue to test and adjust the flour until the gnocchi stay intact in the water and float to the top when cooked. Try not to overwork the dough.

Lightly dust the ball of dough with flour, cover with plastic wrap, and set aside to rest for 5 minutes.

Line a rimmed baking sheet with parchment paper and lightly dust with flour.

Cut off a 4-ounce chunk of the dough, keeping the rest covered. Roll the chunk into a rope about ¾ inch thick, then cut the rope into ¾-inch-long nuggets and dust with flour.

At this point, the gnocchi are ready to cook, but if you'd like to give them the traditional gnocchi shape, roll each nugget down the back of the tines of a table fork (or down a gnocchi board) to form ridges. Dust the gnocchi with flour and lay them in a single layer on the prepared baking sheet. Repeat with the remaining dough, working with 4 ounces at a time. When all the gnocchi have been formed, refrigerate until ready to cook, but no more than a couple of hours (see BBQ Bits & Pieces) or place in the freezer for about an hour or until frozen, then transfer the individual pieces to a resealable plastic bag and store, labeled and frozen, for up to 3 months. Frozen gnocchi will take about 4 minutes to cook.

BBQ BITS & PIECES: 00 flour is soft wheat Italian flour used for pizza doughs and pasta. The number refers to the milling with 00 being the finest texture. It can be replaced with all-purpose flour, but the result will be a somewhat tougher dough. It is available at Italian groceries, many supermarkets, or online.

Note that the gnocchi should be cooked within a couple of hours after they are made. If refrigerated too long, they will become gummy and sticky and unusable. Fortunately, they freeze very well.

There is no rule that says you can't buy potato gnocchi, but homemade is so, so much better. However, it is important that you have the right tools to make that happen, especially a potato ricer. They are inexpensive and available from most home goods stores, specialty kitchenware stores, and online.

SMOKED AND GRILLED HERITAGE PORK CHOP WITH PEACH–HABANERO JAM

Between the brining, smoking, grilling, and glazing, you will create a tender, deliciously flavored pork chop. When cooking a plain pork chop at home—no smoking or grilling—the brining process should always be done. It ensures a tender chop. The smoke does add that indefinable extra something to the chops, but if you choose to eliminate that step, brine and grill as directed (you may have to grill the chops for a bit longer than specified).

A perfect meal might be this chop, Utica Greens (page 194), and Fugate's Firecracker Onions (page 215)!

SERVES 6

Pat the chops dry with paper towels and place them in a large nonreactive container with a lid or an extra-large resealable plastic bag. Add the brine, taking care that it covers the meat entirely. Transfer to the refrigerator and let brine for at least 1 hour or up to 8 hours.

Remove the chops from the refrigerator and drain off all the brine. Pat the chops dry with paper towels and evenly dust both sides of the chops with the seasoning. Set aside to rest at room temperature for 30 minutes.

While the chops are resting, using cherry wood, preheat your smoker to 250°F.

Place the chops in the smoker, away from the heat source. Smoke for 30 minutes or until the internal temperature reaches 100°F. Remove the chops from the smoker and set aside to rest.

While the chops are resting, clean and oil the grill grate and preheat the grill, setting up high- and low-heat zones (see pages 130–131).

6 (16-ounce) bone-in pork chops

1 gallon Standard Brine (page 69)

1 cup All-Purpose Barbecue Seasoning (page 44)

1 cup Peach-Habanero Jam (page 179)

ooo continued

Place the chops in the high-heat zone, putting them all in the same direction at a 45-degree angle to the vertical grate, and grill for 2 minutes. Turn the chops 90 degrees on an unused section of the high-heat side (to get the desired perfect grill marks) and grill for an additional 2 minutes. Turn the chops, placing them as above on another unused section of the high-heat zone, and repeat the process on the second side.

When both sides are beautifully marked, transfer the chops to the low-heat zone of the grill and spoon a dollop of the jam onto each chop. Close the lid and grill for another 5 minutes or until the internal temperature reaches 145°F and the chops are nicely glazed. Remove the chops from the grill and transfer to a large serving platter. Set aside to rest for 5 minutes.

Using a sharp knife, cut the chops into thin slices against the grain (see page 136). Serve immediately, with the remaining jam on the side.

PEACH-HABANERO JAM

MAKES 3 CUPS

Combine the sugar with the pectin in a small bowl and stir to blend completely. The sugar will help prevent the pectin from clumping when added to liquid. Set aside.

Combine the peach puree and peach nectar in a medium saucepan. Stir in the brown sugar, bell pepper, lemon juice, vinegar, seasoning, salt, black pepper, habanero powder, and allspice. Bring to a boil over medium-high heat, stirring frequently. Reduce the heat to maintain a simmer and whisk in the pectin-sugar mixture. Raise the heat and bring back to a boil, stirring frequently, and boil for about 15 minutes or until the jam has thickened with tightly formed bubbles rising to the surface.

Remove from the heat and scrape into a food-safe container. Set aside to cool, then cover and store in the refrigerator until ready to use, up to 2 months.

¼ cup granulated sugar

2 teaspoons apple pectin (see page 60)

1 cup pureed canned peaches

¾ cup peach nectar

½ cup light brown sugar

¼ cup finely diced red bell pepper

2 tablespoons fresh lemon juice

1 tablespoon apple cider vinegar

1 tablespoon All-Purpose Barbecue Seasoning (page 44)

¼ teaspoon kosher salt

⅛ teaspoon ground black pepper

Pinch of habanero chile powder (see page 60)

Pinch of ground allspice

SHANE'S "PASTRAMEN"

This is one of Shane's favorite after-work meals. It combines some barbecue with traditional Asian flavors to make a sensational ramen. The eggs are known as 5-minute eggs—the timing creates a set white with a jiggly, molten yolk, perfect to garnish the soup.

This recipe makes a bit more broth than you need for the recipe, but it freezes well, and it is terrific to have on hand when you feel the need to create a nourishing, flavorful bowl of ramen. If you are a big ramen fan, you can easily double the broth recipe. It can also be used as the base for other soups or braises.

SERVES 6

3 large eggs, at room temperature

3 quarts Pork Broth for Ramen (page 182)

2 tablespoons Kadoya hot sesame oil (see page 183)

2 tablespoons soy sauce, or to taste

2 (10-ounce) packages ramen noodles

2 (6-ounce) cans bamboo shoots, well drained

1 pound pastrami, cut into small cubes

6 scallions, cut into small pieces

3 heads baby bok choy, split in half lengthwise and blanched (see page 183)

2 sheets dried nori seaweed

2 tablespoons pickled ginger

Tare Sauce (page 183)

Bring 1 quart water to a boil in a medium saucepan over high heat, then immediately and carefully lower the eggs into it. Reduce the heat and simmer for 5 minutes. Meanwhile, fill a large bowl with ice and water.

After 5 minutes, using a slotted spoon, lift the eggs from the pot and place them in the ice water to cool them quickly. When cool, carefully peel the eggs and set aside.

Bring the broth to a boil in a large saucepan over high heat. Add the sesame oil and soy sauce and return to a boil. Immediately reduce the heat to very low and keep warm while you finish the dish.

Bring 1 gallon water to a boil in a large saucepan over high heat. Add the ramen noodles and cook according to the manufacturer's directions. Drain in a fine-mesh sieve.

Place an equal portion of the noodles, bamboo shoots, and pastrami in each of six large soup bowls. Ladle an equal portion of the broth into each bowl.

Gently slice each egg in half lengthwise. Garnish each bowl with an egg half, scallions, a bok choy half, a piece of nori, and some of the pickled ginger. Drizzle 1 teaspoon of the tare sauce over each bowl and serve immediately.

PORK BROTH FOR RAMEN

MAKES 4 QUARTS

1 ham hock

3 pounds chicken wings

1 pound smoked pork neck bones

½ pound chicken feet

½ cup Japanese-style soy sauce

¼ sheet kombu

10 dried shiitake mushrooms

½ head garlic, unpeeled, cut in half crosswise

1 medium Spanish onion, charred

1 bunch scallions

2 tablespoons chopped fresh ginger

Place the ham hocks, wings, neck bones, and chicken feet in a large stockpot. Add the soy sauce and 2 gallons cold water. Add the kombu, mushrooms, garlic, onion, scallions, and ginger and bring to a boil over high heat.

Reduce the heat to maintain a gentle simmer and cook, skimming frequently, for 2½ to 3 hours or until deeply flavored. Remove from the heat and strain through a fine-mesh sieve into a food-safe container. Discard all the solids. Set aside to cool completely.

When cool, pour into food-safe containers, cover, and store in the refrigerator until ready to use. The broth may also be frozen for up to 6 months.

NDWICHES, SNACKS

SANDWICHES

Double-Brined Fried Chicken Sandwich

Chef Jeff Brisket Sandwich

Barbecue Lamb Gyro

Tasso-Spiced Bacon BLT with Gochujang
        Ranch Dressing

Bangkok Banger Banh Mi

BBQBANO

The Mobster

SNACKS

Pig Beach Ham Salad Deviled Eggs

Pulled Pork Arancini

Secret Spice Pecan Candied Bacon

Pig Beach Barbecue Kettle Corn

Pigs 'n' Donuts with Jeff's Pepps and
        World Champion Mustard Sauce

Smoked Cheddar Gougères

Barbecue-Flavored Granola

GOWANUS GREENS, AKA PIG BEACH COLLARDS

The Gowanus Canal runs right in front of Pig Beach in Brooklyn, so we often attach its name to dishes we do. These collards are deeply flavorful with a bit more add-ins than the traditional Southern dish. They are even better if you throw in bits and pieces of leftover brisket!

SERVES 6 TO 8

Place a large heavy-bottomed saucepan over medium heat. Add the bacon and oil and cook, stirring frequently, for about 10 minutes or until the bacon is crisp and its fat has rendered.

Add the garlic and cook, stirring frequently, for about 4 minutes or until the garlic is golden brown and very aromatic. Add the onion and cook, stirring frequently, for about 5 minutes or until the onion is soft and translucent.

Add the collards, about 4½ cups of the stock, the vinegar, hot sauce, soy sauce, Worcestershire, and chicken base and stir to blend well. Bring the mixture to a boil, then reduce the heat to maintain a gentle simmer and cook for about 3 hours or until the collards are very soft and tender. You may need to add the additional 1 cup stock to maintain a nice, corn-bread-sopping broth.

Remove from the heat and serve.

3 slices bacon, diced

2 teaspoons vegetable oil

1 tablespoon chopped garlic

1½ cups diced white onion

2 pounds collard greens, well washed, dried, and cut into shreds

5½ cups chicken stock or low-sodium chicken broth

⅓ cup apple cider vinegar

¼ cup Frank's RedHot hot sauce

2 tablespoons soy sauce

2 tablespoons Worcestershire sauce

1 tablespoon Better Than Bouillon roasted chicken base (see page 46)

UTICA GREENS

Utica greens are a staple found in almost every mom-and-pop restaurant in upstate New York where Matt grew up. It is a classic Italian American dish typically prepared with salami and other salumi, but we love the flavor of smoke, so bacon is a substitute for the traditional meats. It gives you all that great flavor of a salted and cured meat, but with the addition of the deep aroma of smoke and fire. Although we do have the traditional collards on the menu, we always have these greens, too.

SERVES 4 TO 6

2 tablespoons olive oil, plus more for greasing

½ teaspoon kosher salt, plus more as needed

1 large head escarole

1 cup Italian seasoned bread crumbs

½ cup finely grated Parmesan cheese

½ cup extra-virgin olive oil

½ cup diced bacon

6 garlic cloves, sliced

1 small white onion, diced

3 to 6 hot cherry peppers, seeded and chopped

½ teaspoon ground black pepper

Crusty Italian bread, for serving

Preheat the oven to 425°F. Lightly coat an 8 x 8-inch square baking pan with olive oil.

Bring a large pot of salted water to a boil over high heat. (The water should be salted enough to taste like the ocean.)

Using a sharp knife, cut the escarole into 1-inch-wide strips.

Fill the clean kitchen sink with very cold water, add the escarole, and aggressively wash it to remove all the dirt and sand. Drain and repeat this process until the water is completely clean. Remove the escarole from the water and shake off as much water as you can.

Add the escarole to the boiling water and blanch for 2 minutes or until just barely wilted with a bit of texture remaining. Meanwhile, fill a large bowl with ice and water.

Using a slotted spoon, transfer the blanched escarole to the ice water to cool it immediately. When cool, using your hands, lift the greens from the ice water and squeeze out as much water as you can. Set aside.

Place the bread crumbs, Parmesan, and olive oil in a medium bowl and toss to blend completely. Set aside.

Heat the extra-virgin olive oil in an extra-large skillet over medium heat. Add the bacon and cook, stirring frequently, for about 10 minutes or until the bacon is crisp and its fat has rendered.

ooo continued

Add the garlic and cook, stirring frequently, for about 4 minutes or until the garlic is golden brown and very aromatic. Add the onion and cook, stirring frequently, for about 5 minutes or until the onion is soft and translucent.

Add the blanched escarole, breaking it up as you add it. Add the cherry peppers and cook for about 5 minutes, tossing and turning to coat the escarole and allow the flavors to blend.

Add about half of the bread crumb mixture to the escarole, season with the salt and black pepper, and stir to combine. Transfer the escarole mixture to the prepared baking pan and top with the remaining bread crumb mixture and transfer to the oven.

Bake for about 15 minutes or until the top is golden brown. Remove from the oven and serve—with crusty Italian bread, of course!

LEGENDARY BAKED BEANS

Even when you are pressed for time, this is one easy recipe to expand your barbecue sides. Since you use canned beans, the cooking time is cut by hours. Baked beans are a great vessel to use up any leftover barbecue scraps. Once the beans have come to a simmer, throw in brisket ends, pulled pork leftovers, or even some diced-up cooked sausage or pulled chicken. It's a great way to jazz them up by adding a hint of barbecue goodness.

SERVES 6 TO 8

Heat the oil in a large saucepan over medium heat. Add the bacon and cook, stirring frequently, for about 10 minutes or until the bacon is crisp and its fat has rendered.

Add the garlic, onion, bell pepper, and jalapeño and cook, stirring frequently, for about 5 minutes or until the vegetables have softened and are very aromatic.

Stir in the baked beans, black-eyed peas, black beans, ketchup, apple juice, sugar, molasses, seasoning, hot sauce, vinegar, mustard, salt, and black pepper and bring to a simmer. Cook at a gentle simmer for 10 minutes.

At this point, you can serve the beans as they are, or you can smoke them before serving. If smoking, using cherry wood, preheat your smoker to 250°F.

Transfer the entire pot to the smoker, uncovered, and smoke for about 40 minutes to get the deep, smoky flavor of traditional baked beans.

1 teaspoon vegetable oil

4 slices bacon, diced

1 garlic clove, minced

1 cup diced white onion

2 tablespoons diced green bell pepper

1 tablespoon finely diced jalapeño

1 (28-ounce) can baked beans

1 (15.5-ounce) can black-eyed peas, drained and rinsed

1 (15.5-ounce) can black beans, drained and rinsed

1 cup ketchup

½ cup apple juice

2 tablespoons dark brown sugar

1 tablespoon molasses

1 tablespoon All-Purpose Barbecue Seasoning (page 44)

1 tablespoon Frank's RedHot hot sauce

1 tablespoon apple cider vinegar

2 teaspoons yellow mustard

1 teaspoon kosher salt

½ teaspoon ground black pepper

GRANDMA RUTH'S SMOKY EGGPLANT PUREE

Smoky eggplant puree, also known as baba ghanoush, traditionally gets its smoky flavor from the roasting of the eggplant, traditionally in a wood-fired oven or on a grill of some type. So why not put it in the smoker? Especially if the smoker is already fired up. Smoking the eggplant won't create the charred, roasted taste of the traditional dish, but you will achieve a deep, smoky deliciousness. Matt is half Lebanese and half Italian, so being able to take traditional and quite nostalgic recipes like baba ghanoush, as prepared by his mom and grandmother, and then tweak them to add another level of flavor, is an inspiration to all our crew.

This dish is a great accompaniment to any barbecue. It's also a terrific vegetarian option for those who may not be as carnivorous as we are!

SERVES 4 TO 6

2 large eggplants (see BBQ Bits & Pieces)

3 tablespoons extra-virgin olive oil

1 teaspoon kosher salt

1 teaspoon ground black pepper

2 garlic cloves, peeled

½ cup strained fresh lemon juice

¼ cup tahini paste

1 tablespoon chopped fresh flat-leaf parsley

Pita bread and smoked meats, for serving (optional)

Using a sharp knife, cut the eggplants in half lengthwise. Season the cut sides with 1 tablespoon of the olive oil, the salt, and the pepper. Set aside to absorb the seasonings for 15 minutes.

Using cherry wood, preheat your smoker to 250°F.

Place the eggplant halves cut-side up in a disposable aluminum pan large enough to hold them. Transfer the pan to the smoker, sitting it away from the heat source. Smoke the eggplant for 45 minutes.

Remove the pan from the smoker and completely enclose the pan in aluminum foil. Return the pan to the smoker and smoke for an additional 45 minutes or until the eggplant is tender and beginning to collapse into itself. Remove the pan from the smoker and place it on a wire rack to cool to room temperature.

SHANE'S GRANDMA'S BREAD & BUTTER PICKLES

The title says it all! These are the pickles Shane grew up eating and they have found a big following at Pig Beach. We think Grandma would be very proud of her legacy.

MAKES 1½ QUARTS

Combine the cucumbers and onion in a medium bowl. Add the salt and toss to coat. Cover and refrigerate for at least 2 hours or up to 4 hours.

Meanwhile, prepare the brine: Combine the cider and white vinegars with the water in a nonreactive medium saucepan. Stir in the sugar, cloves, mustard seeds, coriander, turmeric, chile flakes, and celery seeds and bring to a boil over medium heat. Remove from the heat and strain into a nonreactive container. Discard the solids. Cool to room temperature.

Remove the cucumber mixture from the refrigerator and pour it into a colander. Rinse under cold running water to remove excess salt. Drain well and return to the bowl.

Pour the cooled brine over the cucumber mixture. Cover with plastic wrap and refrigerate for at least 8 hours or up to 24 hours before using.

When fully brined, you can transfer the pickles to jars, taking care that they are submerged in brine, cover, and refrigerate until ready to use, up to 1 month.

2 pounds Kirby cucumbers, washed, trimmed, and cut crosswise into ¼-inch-thick slices

1 large Spanish onion, cut crosswise into thin slices

¼ cup kosher salt

1½ cups apple cider vinegar

½ cup distilled white vinegar

½ cup water

1¾ cups sugar

6 to 8 whole cloves

1 tablespoon yellow mustard seeds

2 teaspoons coriander seeds

1 teaspoon ground turmeric

1 teaspoon chile flakes

½ teaspoon celery seeds

SIDES, SANDWICHES, AND SNACKS

PICKLED RED ONIONS

Pickled red onions are a wonderful addition to your pantry. They make a terrific garnish for all types of barbecue, are tasty on a sandwich or in a salad, and are a perfect addition to a charcuterie plate.

MAKES 2 CUPS

2 large red onions, sliced crosswise into rings

1 cup water

½ cup rice vinegar

¼ cup sugar

2 tablespoons kosher salt

1 tablespoon pickling spice

Place the onion rings in a nonreactive heatproof container. Set aside.

Combine the water, vinegar, sugar, salt, and pickling spice in a nonreactive medium saucepan. Bring to a boil over high heat. Immediately reduce the heat to maintain a gentle simmer and cook for 5 minutes.

Strain the liquid over the onions, discarding the solids. Cover the onions with plastic wrap and set aside to cool in the pickling liquid.

When cool, transfer to a nonreactive container, cover, and store in the refrigerator for up to 1 week.

BARBECUED LAMB GYRO

This is another of Matt's favorites as it reflects his Lebanese roots. He grew up eating gyros, the classic Middle Eastern sandwich made with beef or lamb and served on or with pita (or other flat bread), garnished with onions, tomatoes, and, often, yogurt sauce. All the traditional flavors are in the Pig Beach version, but the smoke intensifies them.

If you don't care for lamb, it can be replaced with any ground meat or a combination of ground meats. The meat mix makes a 1½-pound meatloaf that Matt calls his "smoked gyro meatloaf."

SERVES 6 TO 8

Line a rimmed baking sheet with parchment paper.

Place 2 tablespoons of the oil in a large skillet over medium heat. Add the garlic and cook, stirring frequently, for about 2 minutes or until golden brown but not burned. Stir in the onion and cook for another 4 minutes or until the onion is soft and translucent. Scrape the cooked aromatics onto the prepared baking sheet, spreading them out in an even layer. Transfer to the refrigerator for about 30 minutes or until completely cool.

Using hickory wood, preheat your smoker to 250°F.

Place the lamb and beef along with the spice mix in the bowl of a stand mixer fitted with the paddle attachment. Add the cooled aromatics and beat on low speed for about 5 minutes or until the mixture is completely blended and slightly tacky. (If you want to serve this as a meatloaf, it will yield a 1½-pound loaf.)

Spray a disposable medium aluminum pan with nonstick spray. Scrape the meat mixture from the mixer bowl into the prepared pan and, using your hands, form it into a loaf that is no more than 2 inches high and 4 inches wide.

Place a thermometer probe in the center of the meatloaf and place the meatloaf in the smoker. Smoke for about 1½ hours

3 tablespoons vegetable oil

3 tablespoons minced garlic

1 cup small-dice white onion

1½ pounds ground lamb

½ pound ground beef

6 tablespoons Gyro Spice Mix (page 219)

Nonstick vegetable oil spray

6 to 9 pocketless pita breads

2 cups shredded iceberg lettuce

1 cup Pickled Red Onions (page 210)

NYC White Sauce (page 58), for serving

Summer Vibes HOT Barbecue Sauce (page 219), for serving

ooo continued

or until the internal temperature reaches 155°F. Remove the pan from the smoker and place a piece of parchment paper over the meatloaf. Set another disposable aluminum pan of the same size right-side up on top of the parchment-covered meatloaf. Place a few heavy cans (28-ounce cans of tomatoes work) in the top pan and gently press down to flatten the meatloaf slightly. Transfer the pans to the refrigerator and let rest for at least 4 hours or up to 8 hours.

Remove the pans from the refrigerator. Uncover the meatloaf and discard any fat or liquid in the pan. You can now proceed with the recipe or tightly wrap the meatloaf with plastic wrap and refrigerate for up to 2 days.

When ready to make the sandwiches, preheat the oven to 250°F.

Wrap the pita breads in aluminum foil and place into the preheated oven to warm.

Remove the meatloaf from the refrigerator. Using a sharp knife, cut the loaf crosswise into ¼-inch-thick slices.

Heat the remaining 1 tablespoon oil in a griddle or cast-iron skillet over medium heat. When the oil begins to ripple, add the meatloaf slices, taking care that they are lying flat, and cook, turning once, for about 1 minute or just until heated through and golden brown. If the pan is hot enough, the meat should sizzle immediately when it hits the surface. As the slices are heated, transfer to a platter, cover with aluminum foil, and keep warm.

Remove the pita from the oven. Unwrap the breads and place each on a warmed plate. Top with an equal portion of the gyro meat followed by the iceberg lettuce and pickled onions. Drizzle with the white sauce and then the barbecue sauce.

Fold each pita in half to enclose the filling and serve immediately.

GYRO SPICE MIX

MAKES 6 TABLESPOONS

Combine the za'atar, seasoning blend, salt, and chile flakes in a small bowl and stir to blend completely.

Transfer to a food-safe container, cover, and store in a cool, dark spot until ready to use, up to 3 months.

2 tablespoons za'atar (see BBQ Bits & Pieces)

2 tablespoons Greek Seasoning Blend (see page 113)

2 tablespoons kosher salt

¼ teaspoon chile flakes

SUMMER VIBES HOT BARBECUE SAUCE

MAKES ABOUT 2½ CUPS

Place the ketchup and mustard in a medium bowl. Add the white and cider vinegars and whisk to blend. Add the sugar, turmeric, salt, cayenne, onion, and garlic and stir until very well blended.

Transfer to a food-safe container, cover, and store in the refrigerator until ready to use, up to 1 month.

2 cups ketchup

½ cup yellow mustard

½ cup white vinegar

2 tablespoons apple cider vinegar

2 tablespoons sugar

1 tablespoon ground turmeric

1 tablespoon kosher salt

1½ teaspoons cayenne pepper

1 teaspoon granulated onion

1 teaspoon granulated garlic

BBQ BITS & PIECES: Za'atar is a deeply flavorful Middle Eastern herb and spice mix that is used to season braises, breads, and salads. It is available from specialty food stores, some super-markets, and online.

SIDES, SANDWICHES, AND SNACKS

TASSO-SPICED BACON BLT WITH GOCHUJANG RANCH DRESSING

This is not an ordinary diner BLT! The recipe looks long and complicated, but it's really just the time it takes to cure the pork belly that makes it seem harder than it is. The spice mix and the fatty pork belly unite to make a sensational bite.

A fun twist in this recipe is the addition of gochujang (see page 64) to the ranch dressing. Gochujang is an important ingredient in Korean cuisine, but it also really kicks up the umami of any dish.

SERVES 8

5 pounds skin-off pork belly

2 cups Tasso Spice Mix (opposite)

1 teaspoon vegetable oil

16 slices marble rye or sourdough bread

Kosher salt and ground black pepper

1 cup

Gochujang Buttermilk Ranch Dressing (page 64)

2 large heirloom tomatoes, cored, peeled, and cut crosswise into 16 thin slices

4 cups baby arugula

Place the pork belly in a large nonreactive container. Add the spice mix and turn to season all sides. Cover and refrigerate for at least 1 week, turning occasionally.

When ready to smoke, remove the pork belly from the refrigerator. Take it out of the container and set aside for about 20 minutes or until it has come to room temperature.

Using cherry or apple wood, preheat your smoker to 250°F.

Place the pork belly in the smoker fat-side up, away from the heat source. Smoke for 5 hours or until the internal temperature reaches 198° to 203°F.

Line a rimmed baking sheet large enough to hold the pork belly with parchment paper.

Remove the pork belly from the smoker and transfer to the prepared baking sheet. Refrigerate for at least 8 hours. If you want the belly to have a uniform shape, place a piece of parchment paper on top of the meat. Place another baking sheet of the same size over the parchment-covered pork belly. Place a few heavy cans (28-ounce cans of tomatoes work) onto the top pan and gently press down to flatten the belly slightly. Transfer the pans to the refrigerator and let rest for at least 4 hours or up to 8 hours.

When ready to cook, remove the meat from the refrigerator. It should be cold and very firm. Uncover and cut crosswise into thin slices as for bacon.

Heat the oil in a cast-iron skillet or griddle over medium heat. When very hot, add the pork belly slices, a few at a time, and fry, turning once, for about 2 minutes or until golden brown and crisp. Transfer to a wire rack and repeat to cook the remaining slices. Pour off and save all the rendered fat as you fry.

Using some of the rendered fat, grease a griddle. Working with a few slices at a time, place the bread into the hot grease and toast, turning occasionally, for about 3 minutes or until golden brown. Season with a little salt and set aside as you toast the remaining bread.

When all the bread has been toasted, place 8 slices on a cutting board. Slather about 1 tablespoon of the ranch dressing on each slice. Top each with about 4 slices of the pork belly, followed by 2 slices of tomato. Season the tomato with salt and pepper and top each sandwich with about ½ cup of the arugula. Drizzle with the remaining ranch and top with a second piece of the toast. Using a serrated knife, cut the sandwiches in half on the diagonal and serve immediately.

TASSO SPICE MIX

MAKES 2 CUPS

Combine the salt, paprika, and garlic in a medium bowl. Add the black pepper, sugar, Cure Number 1, white pepper, onion, Sichuan pepper, thyme, cayenne, oregano, allspice, and cinnamon and stir to blend completely.

Transfer to a nonreactive container, cover, and store at room temperature for no more than 2 days before using.

1 cup kosher salt

½ cup paprika

⅓ cup chopped garlic

3 tablespoons ground black pepper

2 tablespoons light brown sugar

1 tablespoon Cure Number 1 (see page 88)

1 tablespoon ground white pepper

1 tablespoon granulated onion

2 teaspoons ground Sichuan pepper

2 teaspoons dried thyme

1 teaspoon cayenne pepper

1 teaspoon dried oregano

1 teaspoon ground allspice

1 teaspoon ground cinnamon

SECRET SPICE PECAN CANDIED BACON

This dish was a favorite at our late, lamented Manhattan restaurant, Pig Bleecker. Although it is not barbecued, the smoked bacon resonates, creating a sweet, salty, smoky irresistible snack. It is easy to prepare and the perfect accompaniment to a cold libation!

SERVES 4 TO 6

Preheat the oven to 350°F. Line a rimmed baking sheet with aluminum foil. Place a wire rack on top of the foil.

Place the bacon slices on the rack, keeping them straight and separated. Bake for about 15 minutes or until the bacon is about three-quarters cooked. You don't want it to be crisp.

While the bacon is cooking, combine the sugar, pecans, pepper, and allspice in a food processor. Process, using quick on-and-off pulses, just until the nuts are finely chopped.

Remove the bacon from the oven. Do not turn the oven off. Carefully sprinkle an even layer of the pecan mixture over each slice, then gently spritz with the all-purpose spritz. This will help the sugar melt and caramelize during the final baking.

Return the pan to the oven and bake for another 10 to 15 minutes or until the sugar has caramelized and the bacon is crisp.

Remove the candied bacon from the oven and transfer to a serving platter. Set aside to cool to room temperature. As the bacon cools, the caramelized coating will also crisp. If you don't transfer it from the rack before it cools, the sugars will harden and it will be difficult to remove. If this happens, transfer the rack back to the hot oven to warm for a minute or two so that the bacon can easily release.

12 to 14 slices fine-quality smoked bacon (about a 1-pound package)

½ cup packed light brown sugar

½ cup chopped pecans

½ teaspoon ground black pepper

¼ teaspoon ground allspice

¼ cup All-Purpose Barbecue Spritz (page 68)

PIG BEACH BARBECUE KETTLE CORN

Movie night? Cocktail party? Casual get-together? This popcorn will be the treat of the event! Packed into a resealable themed plastic bag and tied with a colorful ribbon, it also makes a unique house or holiday gift.

SERVES 4 TO 6

¼ cup vegetable oil

½ cup popcorn kernels

¼ cup All-Purpose Barbecue Seasoning (page 44)

1 teaspoon kosher salt

Place the oil in a large, heavy-bottomed saucepan or Dutch oven. Add the popcorn kernels, cover, and set over medium-high heat. Cook, shaking the pot occasionally, until you hear popping sounds, then continue shaking the pot until the popping begins to slow down; popping will become very rapid and then slow down over the course of 5 to 8 minutes. Remove the pot from the heat. Do not uncover. Set aside for a minute or two to allow the popping to completely stop.

Transfer the popped corn to a large serving bowl and immediately sprinkle with the barbecue seasoning and salt. Toss to coat well. Serve immediately, or transfer to a food-safe container with a lid or large resealable plastic bag, cover (or seal the bag), and store at room temperature for up to 1 week.

PIGS 'N' DONUTS WITH JEFF'S PEPPS AND WORLD CHAMPION MUSTARD SAUCE

The slightly sweet dough encasing the snappy, spicy cocktail franks has to be one of our kitchen's greatest inventions. Once you try Pigs 'n' Donuts, you'll serve them at every gathering. We always have the mustard sauce and Jeff's Pepps on hand, but if you don't, serve them with your favorite mustard and spicy condiment.

SERVES 6

Place the milk in a small saucepan and warm over low heat until it reaches 90° to 100°F. Whisk in the yeast and sugar and let sit for 1 minute or until you see small bubbles forming. Remove from the heat and pour the mixture into the bowl of a stand mixer fitted with the dough hook.

Add the flour, baking powder, and salt and begin beating on low. Add 1 of the eggs and the shortening and beat until well incorporated. Continue beating for about 10 minutes or until a smooth, silky dough has formed. Cover the bowl with plastic wrap and set aside in a warm spot to rise for 1 hour or until doubled in size.

When ready to bake, preheat the oven to 400°F. Line a baking sheet with parchment paper.

Place the remaining egg in a small bowl. Add a drop or two of water and whisk to lighten. Set aside.

Lightly flour a clean work surface. Scrape the dough onto it and lightly dust the dough with flour. Using a rolling pin, gently roll the dough out to ¼-inch thickness, then cut the dough into 1 x 2-inch strips. Using a pastry brush, lightly coat each strip with the beaten egg.

Working with one strip at a time, place a cocktail frank in the center of each strip and roll the strip up and around the frank, pushing down slightly to close the seam. The egg will help

¾ cup milk

1 tablespoon active dry yeast

2 tablespoons sugar

2 cups all-purpose flour, plus more for dusting

2 teaspoons baking powder

2 teaspoons kosher salt

2 large eggs, at room temperature

¼ cup vegetable shortening

1 (12-ounce) package cocktail frankfurters

4 tablespoons (½ stick) unsalted butter, melted

Coarse sea salt, for sprinkling

¼ cup thinly sliced scallions

World Champion Mustard Sauce (page 51), for serving

Jeff's Pepps (see page 98), for serving (optional)

keep the dough sealed around the frank during baking. Place the wrapped franks on the prepared baking sheet as you go.

Using a clean pastry brush, lightly coat the top of each one with the melted butter and sprinkle a pinch of coarse salt over the butter. Bake for about 20 minutes or until the dough is puffed and golden brown. Remove from the oven and transfer to a serving plate.

Sprinkle with the sliced scallions and serve piping-hot, with the mustard sauce and Jeff's Pepps, if desired.

SMOKED CHEDDAR GOUGÈRES

Gougères are a traditional French holiday snack, often served with champagne as a predinner *dégustation*. They are classically made with Gruyère cheese, but we've put the barbecue spin on them by using smoked cheddar cheese.

MAKES 24

Preheat the oven to 400°F. Line a baking sheet with parchment paper and spray the parchment with nonstick spray.

Place the milk and butter in a medium saucepan. Bring to a simmer over medium-high heat. Using a wooden spoon, beat in the flour and salt to make a thick batter.

Reduce the heat to medium-low and cook, beating continuously, for about 5 minutes or until the pan is dry and the batter is just beginning to slightly scorch on the bottom.

Immediately remove from the heat and scrape the batter into the bowl of a stand mixer fitted with the paddle attachment. Beat on low speed for about 5 minutes or until all steam has evaporated and you can hold your hands against the side of the bowl without burning.

Add the eggs one at a time, beating on medium to fully incorporate each egg before adding the next. When the last egg has been added, beat for 3 minutes. The batter should be very sticky but quite thick. Add ¾ cup of the cheese and beat to incorporate.

Scrape the batter into a pastry bag fitted with a ½-inch round tip. Pipe the batter into 1-inch rosettes on the prepared baking sheet, leaving about 1 inch between each one. Sprinkle the top of each rosette with a bit of the remaining cheese.

Bake for about 20 minutes or until doubled in size and golden brown. Remove from the oven and allow to cool slightly before serving.

Nonstick vegetable oil spray

1 cup skim milk

½ cup (1 stick) unsalted butter

1 cup all-purpose flour

⅛ teaspoon kosher salt

4 large eggs, at room temperature

1 cup shredded smoked cheddar cheese

BARBECUE-FLAVORED GRANOLA

This is just like a classic healthy breakfast granola with the added hit of barbecue seasoning. It is delicious as a snack or as a breakfast treat with yogurt or milk.

MAKES 8 CUPS

4 cups old-fashioned rolled oats

1 cup smoked pecan pieces

¼ cup hulled sunflower seeds

¼ cup hulled pepitas (pumpkin seeds)

1 tablespoon All-Purpose Barbecue Seasoning (page 44)

1 teaspoon kosher salt

½ cup (1 stick) unsalted butter, melted

¼ cup honey

¼ cup pure maple syrup

¼ cup sweetened shredded coconut

¼ cup dried cherries

¼ cup dried cranberries

¼ cup mini chocolate chips (optional)

Preheat the oven to 350°F.

Combine the oats, pecans, sunflower seeds, pepitas, barbecue seasoning, and salt in a large bowl. Drizzle the butter, honey, and maple syrup over the top and, using your hands, toss to evenly coat.

Scrape the mixture onto a large rimmed baking sheet. Bake for 10 minutes. Remove from the oven and stir in the coconut. Using a rubber spatula, press the granola down onto the baking sheet in an even layer. Return to the oven and bake for an additional 10 minutes. Remove the granola from the oven and place the baking sheet on a wire rack to cool completely. Do not agitate the mix while it is cooling.

When cooled, sprinkle the dried cranberries, cherries, and chocolate chips (if using) over the top. Using your hands, begin breaking up the toasted granola, incorporating the toppings into it.

Transfer to a food-safe container, cover, and store in a cool, dark spot for up to 2 weeks.

AFTER THE MEATS, YOU GOTTA HAVE SWEETS

KAREN'S KEY LIME PIE

Everybody loves key lime pie, and this is a spectacular one. We always use fresh key lime juice, which really does make an amazing difference in the pie's taste. If you can't find key limes, you can use ¼ cup of regular lime juice mixed with 1 tablespoon fresh lemon juice. This will give you that extra tart taste you need.

MAKES ONE 10-INCH PIE

Preheat the oven to 325°F.

Combine the egg yolks and condensed milk in a medium bowl. Add the lime juice and beat to blend completely.

Using a rubber spatula, scrape the mixture into the cooled pie crust. Bake for about 16 minutes or until the filling has set. Remove from the oven and place on a wire rack to cool completely before serving.

Serve garnished with whipped cream, if desired.

4 large egg yolks, at room temperature	**1 (10-inch) Graham Cracker Pie Crust (recipe follows)**
1 (28-ounce) can sweetened condensed milk	**Whipped cream, for serving (optional)**
¼ cup fresh key lime juice	

GRAHAM CRACKER PIE CRUST

MAKES 1 (10-INCH) PIE CRUST

Preheat the oven to 350°F.

Combine the graham cracker crumbs, pecans, sugar, cinnamon, and salt in a medium bowl. Add the melted butter and, using a wooden spoon, mix to blend thoroughly.

Transfer the crumb mixture to a 9-inch pie dish. Using your fingertips, press the mixture over the bottom and up the sides of the pie dish, taking care to smooth around the edge of the dish.

Bake for about 12 minutes or until the crust is lightly colored and very fragrant. Remove from the oven and place on a wire rack to cool completely before filling.

¾ cup graham cracker crumbs	**1 teaspoon ground cinnamon**
½ cup finely chopped pecans	**⅛ teaspoon kosher salt**
3 tablespoons dark brown sugar	**6 tablespoons (¾ stick) unsalted butter, melted**

BUCKEYES

Buckeyes are named for their resemblance to the buckeye, a nut from a horse chestnut tree native to Ohio. They are easy to make and a great way to introduce kids to cooking. The combination of peanut butter and chocolate is one that seems to be everyone's favorite combo.

MAKES 24 TO 30

2¼ cups confectioners' sugar

1 cup smooth peanut butter

⅓ cup unsalted butter, at room temperature

1 tablespoon coconut oil

1 teaspoon pure vanilla extract

¼ teaspoon kosher salt

1 cup chocolate chips

¼ cup unsalted peanuts (optional)

1 tablespoon coarse sea salt (optional)

Line a rimmed baking sheet with parchment paper.

Place the confectioners' sugar in the bowl of a stand mixer fitted with the paddle attachment. Add the peanut butter, butter, coconut oil, vanilla, and salt. Mix on low to just combine, then raise the speed to medium and beat until a smooth, firm dough forms.

Using a tablespoon, form 1-tablespoon balls of dough, placing them on the prepared baking sheet as you go. Transfer the baking sheet to the refrigerator for at least 30 minutes to chill and firm up.

When ready to dip the balls, place the chocolate chips in a microwavable bowl and microwave on high for 30 seconds or until the chips are about three-quarters melted. Remove from the microwave and stir until all the chips have melted. (Alternatively, melt the chocolate chips in a heatproof bowl set over a saucepan of boiling water; this will probably take about 1 minute over boiling water.)

Remove the peanut butter balls from the refrigerator. Working with one at a time, stick a sturdy toothpick or a thin skewer into the center and, holding the toothpick, quickly and evenly dip the ball into the chocolate to about halfway up its side. If desired, either press a peanut into the top center or sprinkle with a bit of coarse sea salt. Return the chocolate-coated ball to the baking sheet and repeat until all the balls are coated. Refrigerate for at least 30 minutes or until the chocolate has hardened before serving.

Serve or transfer to a covered container. Place in a single layer, cover, and store in the refrigerator for up to 1 week.

CHOCOLATE-PECAN BARS

Derby pie is closely associated with the running of the Kentucky Derby so, to us, it is a necessary dessert on a barbecue menu. But rather than make this rich, chocolaty, nutty dessert as a pie, we've turned it into handheld bars. Easier to serve and REALLY easy to eat!

MAKES ABOUT 18 BARS

To prepare the crust, preheat the oven to 350°F. Lightly spray a 9 x 13-inch baking dish with nonstick spray.

Combine the graham cracker crumbs, melted butter, sugars, and cinnamon in a medium bowl. Add the egg white and stir to blend completely.

Using your fingertips, press the crumb mixture into the prepared baking dish, taking care that the bottom is an even layer. Use the palms of your hands to press it down. Bake for about 10 minutes or just until lightly colored and set. Remove from the oven and set aside to cool.

While the crust is cooling, prepare the filling: Place the eggs in a large bowl. Add the sugar, corn syrup, melted butter, bourbon, heavy cream, vanilla, and salt, whisking to thoroughly blend. Using a rubber spatula, fold in the chocolate chips and pecans.

Pour the mixture onto the cooled crust. Bake for about 40 minutes or until the middle is set and the top is lightly colored. Remove from the heat and place on a wire rack to cool.

When cool, using a serrated knife, cut the cookie into about 18 bars of equal size.

Serve, or store in an airtight container, in layers separated by waxed paper, at room temperature for up to 3 days.

CRUST

Nonstick vegetable oil spray

1½ cups graham cracker crumbs

4 tablespoons (½ stick) unsalted butter, melted

3 tablespoons granulated sugar

1 tablespoon light brown sugar

¼ teaspoon ground cinnamon

1 large egg white, beaten

FILLING

3 large eggs, at room temperature

1 cup packed light brown sugar

1 cup light corn syrup

4 tablespoons (½ stick) unsalted butter, melted

2 teaspoons bourbon

1 tablespoon heavy cream

1 tablespoon pure vanilla extract

¼ teaspoon kosher salt

12 ounces semisweet mini chocolate chips

2 cups chopped pecans

DAD'S APPLE CRISP

This recipe comes from Matt's dad, who loves to mix up his apples. However, if you can't find the four different types, just use whatever apples you like. The crisp will still be delicious.

SERVES 12

CRUMBLE
1 cup all-purpose flour

1 cup apple-cinnamon-flavor instant oatmeal (3 packets)

1 cup packed light brown sugar

1 teaspoon baking powder

½ teaspoon kosher salt

1 cup (2 sticks) chilled unsalted butter, grated (see page 264)

FILLING
1 pound Honeycrisp apples, peeled, cored, and sliced ⅛ inch thick

1 pound Northern Spy apples, peeled, cored, and sliced ⅛ inch thick

1 pound Newtown Pippin apples, peeled, cored, and sliced ⅛ inch thick

1 pound Granny Smith apples, peeled, cored, and sliced ⅛ inch thick

½ cup packed light brown sugar

¼ cup all-purpose flour

1 tablespoon cornstarch

1 teaspoon ground cinnamon

1 teaspoon ground ginger

½ teaspoon ground allspice

½ teaspoon kosher salt

2 tablespoons fresh lemon juice

6 tablespoons (¾ stick) unsalted butter, melted

Vanilla ice cream, frozen yogurt, or whipped cream, for garnish (optional)

Preheat the oven to 350°F.

To make the crumble, combine the flour, oatmeal, brown sugar, baking powder, and salt in a medium bowl. Add the grated butter and, using your hands, work the mixture into a coarse crumble. Set aside.

To make the filling, place the apples in a large bowl. Add the brown sugar, flour, cornstarch, cinnamon, ginger, allspice, and salt and toss to blend well. Sprinkle with the lemon juice, followed by the melted butter, and toss again to coat the apples.

Pour the filling into a 10 x 15-inch baking dish. Spoon the crumble over the apples in an even layer. Bake for 40 minutes or until the apples are bubbling and cooked through and the crumble is golden brown. Remove from the oven and place on a wire rack to cool slightly before serving.

Serve with vanilla ice cream, frozen yogurt, or whipped cream, if desired. Cover leftovers and store in the refrigerator for up to 3 days.

CAST-IRON PEACH-BLUEBERRY COBBLER

We love making this dessert in a big ol' cast-iron skillet. It suits the down-home home cooking that the cobbler represents. Even in the winter, frozen peaches and blueberries will turn this recipe into a delicious end to a meal.

SERVES 12

CRUMBLE

1 cup all-purpose flour

1 cup apple-cinnamon-flavor instant oatmeal (3 packets)

1 cup packed light brown sugar

¾ cup chopped pecans

1 teaspoon baking powder

½ teaspoon kosher salt

1 cup (2 sticks) chilled unsalted butter, grated (see BBQ Bits & Pieces)

FILLING

3 pounds skin-on peaches, pitted and cut into ½-inch-thick wedges (about 8 cups)

½ cup packed light brown sugar

¼ cup all-purpose flour

1 tablespoon cornstarch

1 teaspoon ground cinnamon

1 teaspoon ground ginger

½ teaspoon ground allspice

½ teaspoon kosher salt

2 tablespoons fresh lemon juice

6 tablespoons (¾ stick) unsalted butter, melted

1 pint blueberries

Preheat the oven to 350°F.

To make the crumble, combine the flour, oatmeal, brown sugar, pecans, baking powder, and salt in a medium bowl. Add the grated butter and, using your hands, work the mixture into a coarse crumble. Set aside.

To make the filling, place the peaches in a large bowl. Add the brown sugar, flour, cornstarch, cinnamon, ginger, allspice, and salt and toss to blend well. Sprinkle with the lemon juice, followed by the melted butter, and toss again to coat the peaches. Fold in the blueberries.

Pour the filling into a large well-seasoned cast-iron skillet. Spoon the crumble over the fruit filling in an even layer. Bake for 40 minutes or until the fruit is bubbling and cooked through and the crumble is golden brown.

Serve bubbling-hot, straight from the pan.

BBQ BITS & PIECES: The butter needs to be very cold; once cold, it is easily grated on the large holes of a box grater. The grated pieces are easier to incorporate into the dry mixture.

BARBECUE TIME IS COCKTAIL TIME!

GAMBLER'S CORTEZ

Who doesn't love a margarita? We took that base and spiced it up with a hint of jalapeño and the punch of sweet yuzu. This drink is a year-round staple at Pig Beach.

SERVES 1

2 lime wedges

½ teaspoon jalapeño salt, plus more for the rim (see BBQ Bits & Pieces)

1½ ounces Tanteo jalapeño tequila

1½ ounces yuzu juice (see BBQ Bits & Pieces)

½ ounce fresh lime juice

¼ ounce simple syrup (recipe follows)

Run a lime wedge around the rim of a rocks glass. Fill a saucer or small bowl with jalapeno salt, and dip the wet rim into the dry mixture, twisting gently to evenly coat. Fill the rocks glass with ice cubes. Set aside.

Fill a cocktail shaker with ice. Add the tequila, yuzu juice, lime juice, and simple syrup. Cover and shake for 10 seconds. Pour off any water that has melted into the rocks glass, then strain the cocktail into the glass. Dip the lime wedge into the jalapeño salt and place it on the rim of the glass. Serve immediately.

SIMPLE SYRUP

MAKES ABOUT 1½ CUPS

1 cup water

1 cup sugar

Place the water in a small saucepan. Add the sugar and bring to a simmer over medium heat. Simmer for about 2 minutes, until the sugar has dissolved. Remove from the heat and set aside to cool.

When cool, transfer to a jar or pitcher, cover, and store in the refrigerator for up to 1 month.

BBQ BITS & PIECES: Yuzu is a Japanese citrus fruit that is slightly sweeter than a Persian lime.

Both yuzu juice and jalapeño salt are available at some specialty food stores and online.

FROZÉ

Come summer, this is about the most popular libation at Pig Beach. You can't have just one! Even through the cold winter outdoor dining months, our customers don't allow us to take it off the menu.

SERVES 2

Place the vodka, wine, grapefruit juice, lemonade, simple syrup, Select, and lemon juice in a blender. Add the ice and blend on high for about 1 minute or until the mixture has a slushlike consistency. Divide the frozé evenly among two highball glasses. Garnish each glass with a grapefruit slice and serve immediately.

4 ounces Three Olives grapefruit vodka

2 ounces Day Owl rosé

1½ ounces fresh grapefruit juice

1½ ounces lemonade

1½ ounces simple syrup (see page 268)

¾ ounce Select Aperitivo liqueur

½ ounce fresh lemon juice

2 cups ice

4 half-moon slices fresh grapefruit, about ⅛ inch thick

LOOSE LUCY

Cocktails get their names from people we know, jokes we've told, inebriated nights when anything goes—that's where cocktail names are born. If you are a follower of the Grateful Dead, you'll know this gem of a song title as well.

SERVES 1

Combine the grapefruit juice, vodka, elderflower liqueur, simple syrup, and lime juice in a cocktail shaker filled with ice. Cover and shake to blend thoroughly. Strain the cocktail into a chilled martini glass. Garnish with a lime wedge and serve.

2 ounces fresh grapefruit juice

1½ ounces vodka

½ ounce elderflower liqueur

1 ounce simple syrup (see page 268)

1 ounce fresh lime juice

Lime wedge, for garnish

MERMAID JUICE

This drink takes you right into the middle of summertime tiki cocktails. The classic base of light, dark, and coconut rums tangled up with tropical fruits will get the summer vibes flowing.

SERVES 1

3 ounces pineapple juice

1 ounce fruit punch

1 ounce Flor de Caña white rum

½ ounce Goslings black rum

½ ounce Rumhaven coconut water rum

½ ounce simple syrup (see page 268)

¼ ounce fresh lime juice

1 lime wedge, for garnish (optional)

1 cocktail umbrella, for garnish (optional)

Fill your favorite hurricane or tiki glass with ice. Set aside.

Combine the pineapple juice, fruit punch, Flor de Caña, Goslings, Rumhaven, simple syrup, and lime juice in a cocktail shaker filled with ice. Cover and shake well for 10 seconds. Strain the cocktail into the prepared glass. Garnish with a lime wedge and a cocktail umbrella, if desired, and serve immediately.